Dreams Derailed

Dreams Derailed

Undocumented Youths in the Trump Era

WILLIAM A. SCHWAB

The University of Arkansas Press
Fayetteville
2019

Manufactured in the United States of America

ISBN: 978-1-68226-083-8
eISBN: 978-1-61075-285-5

23 22 21 20 19 5 4 3 2 1

∞ The paper used in this publication meets the minimum requirements of the American National Standard for Permanence of Paper for Printed Library Materials Z39.48-1984.

Library of Congress Control Number: 2018949399

For America's undocumented youth,
who will persevere

CONTENTS

FOREWORD

One of the most enduring and indeed accurate narratives in the American story is that which defines America as a nation of immigrants. It is a truth that can be tested in every dimension, much like a flower in which every individual petal attests to its beauty. It is true, for example, that every national group who settled here since the indigenous people who resided here for thousands of years, migrated from other places in the world. It is also true that immigrants were decisive in populating the country, from the earliest pilgrim colonizers to the first city dwellers to the transcontinental pioneers to the prodigious industrial workers to today's technology innovators and farm and ranch producers. It is verifiable that the waves of immigrants produced sons and daughters who organized some of the nation's largest companies, served in the highest public offices, led the US armed forces, created some of the most evocative art, and shepherded breakthrough inventions and scientific discoveries.

With such an indisputable legacy and with such a profound positive impact, it is perplexing why it is also true that immigration has been one of the greatest sources of contention and even violence across the nation over the last two-and-a-half centuries. In the colonial period, groups of immigrants were considered inferior stock and discriminatory practices limited the work they could do, the places they could live, and the role they could play in public governance. As the nation grew immigrants were segregated by neighborhoods, jobs, wage levels, social standing, admission to select schools, and leadership opportunities. The instruments of restrictive and punitive immigration policies included quotas, harsh temporary labor programs, brutal law enforcement, and ignoring human rights protections.

Despite the harshness of institutional and public attitudes over the decades immigrants have proven to be essential to the functioning of the US economy. Today sectors such as residential construction, agricultural production, food processing and preparation, horticulture, home and office custodial care, home health care, landscaping, public works construction, textile production, and furniture making, could not function in many parts of the nation without immigrants. This economic reality has created push-pull forces. Immigrants are pushed by economic deprivation in their home countries to seek better pay and pulled by the obvious need for workers in the stronger US economy. Other factors such as political instabilities in the sending countries, the educational magnets of American higher education, and family ties to earlier immigrants are also at work. The cumulative result of all these forces is that there are more foreign-born residents in the United States today than at any other point in US history. For some Americans this is a manifestation of a national strength; for others it is a fearsome harbinger of wage-reducing labor surpluses and anxiety-produced cultural change.

The operative consensus in many sectors of our society is that our current immigration laws are broken. And the broad outline of a workable framework for more than a decade has included action on three fronts: border security, a system of legalization for the law-abiding but long-term currently undocumented, and a rigorous but fair path to citizenship. These elements have been recognized as the basic framework by legislators, business leaders, US presidents, immigration advocates, law enforcement officials, and local government leaders, particularly in border regions; but all to no avail. There is national gridlock on immigration reform. The prospects for meaningful improvements in the immigration system ebb and flow with political fortunes, high-profile criminal incidents, and economic cycles. It is a multifaceted, complex, volatile, and intransigent stalemate.

But as is often the case in the matters of public policy there are small corners of the debate that are different. They create exceptions to the well-worn arguments on the table. They are different because facets of their reality are special. Such is the case with the Dreamers, the category of young immigrants who were brought to the United States by their parents as children and who have lived most of their lives knowing only their surroundings in the United States. Most have gone to school here, have never returned to their home country, have learned US civic and cultural mores, and have been prepared to make their economic and societal contributions here. All sides in the debate seem to understand that the Dreamers pose a special case and deserve a more careful and compassionate policy response.

That is why President Obama, after unsuccessfully seeking congressional passage of a solution for the Dreamers, took executive action to create DACA, the Deferred Action for Childhood Arrivals program. Even though the Dreamers constitute only a sliver of the more than twelve million immigrants whose lives hang in the balance of the immigration reform stalemate, the Dreamers have been the flashpoint of one of the hottest and most rancorous partisan battles in recent US political history, and they are emblematic of all of the pain in the present immigration standoff.

For me, this is much more than a political cage match. It is personal. I have seen the plight of the Dreamers up close and know that our present inaction is insupportable and inhumane. My vantage point is shaped by personal experience with real people, such as my experience with a young man named Carlos.

Six years ago, I received a telephone call from a professor at a small community college in East Texas. He told me that a student of his named Carlos had written a paper about my work as mayor of San Antonio for a history course and that it had been selected as the best student paper of the year by a Texas history association. He said he was taking Carlos to present the paper in Houston in a few weeks and they wanted to drive to San Antonio to meet me. I replied that a Sunday lunch would work and I would read his paper before our meeting.

When I read the paper, I concluded it was the best analysis of the economic development strategy I tried to execute as mayor written by any journalist or analyst at any level. So when we met for lunch the following Sunday, I complimented Carlos and told him he had the skills to be a good journalist or writer. He replied that he had his heart set on being an engineer. I asked how prepared he was to study engineering and he told me he had earned straight A's in his math and science courses. I asked him how he planned to make the transition from an East Texas community college to an engineering school and he answered that he honestly had no idea.

I also learned in that lunch that at age nine Carlos had crossed the Rio Grande on an inner tube with his mother. They traveled to North

Texas to join his father and sisters in Dallas, where each parent was soon working two jobs in restaurants. One morning as they drove to work a truck barreled through a red light, T-boned the family car, killed his mother, and disabled his father. Some years later the father and young boy moved to East Texas where the disabled father was offered a food service job. They lived in an aluminum garage with a concrete floor, slept in their car, and showered at a local gym. Despite working long hours in a restaurant, Carlos became a straight-A student.

Before the lunch was over I committed to help him qualify for the engineering program at the University of Texas at San Antonio and to provide him a place to live if he got into the program. The dean of the engineering college told me Carlos was clearly qualified and that he would be admitted as a second-year student that fall. But the dean explained that engineering courses are usually spread out over four years and that the community college Carlos had attended had offered none of the courses. Carlos would have to take up to five engineering courses in certain semesters to complete the curriculum and such a schedule would be an impossible hurdle for even the best-prepared student.

The first year Carlos lived in a guesthouse on our property. I saw his light on until one o'clock or later almost every night as he tackled thermodynamics, fluid mechanics, materials science, systems controls, and other engineering courses. At the end of the first semester he brought home five As. And he did it semester after semester, except for the one when he came with tears in his eyes because he had a C among four As. All this he accomplished while commuting on multiple buses daily, some twenty miles to the campus, for fear that if he drove a car a minor traffic infraction or even a broken taillight could result in deportation.

When President Obama announced DACA, my wife Mary Alice secured an attorney and walked Carlos through the application process. I have never seen a bigger smile on any human being than the day he came from the mailbox with a green card labeled "US Government." Carlos continued to work hard, took courses in an honors program, and graduated after an extra semester. He was selected to be a manufacturing engineer in a San Antonio-based automotive supplier firm and his employer tells me he is a valued member of their team.

I tell his story to describe in human terms what DACA means to people who struggle through adversity and who strive for worthwhile dreams and to provide a sense of who the DACA participants, the Dreamers actually are. Carlos is one; there are eight hundred thousand. Carlos came to the United States at nine years old. His extended family is here. He has never been back, nor does he know anyone in his birthplace of Guanajuato, Mexico. If DACA is not extended the first thing that will happen is that without renewal he will lose his legal status and then he will lose his job. Then he will be subject to deportation. The government already has access to all the personal contact information needed to deport him. He provided it in his DACA application.

I pray that the lessons we will all learn through this DACA process will help us find our way to the broader immigration reforms our country needs. Bill Schwab has provided our nation a major service in filling out the story of the Dreamers and DACA. He has written a book that speaks from his extensive writing and studies, from academic research, and from his policy experiences. More important, Bill speaks from his personal engagement with Dreamers and DACA participants across the nation. He knows the students involved and their parents and families. He has shared their fears, hopes, and now again fears. This is a book about history, about politics, and about law. It is also a book about people, about fairness, and about the future of our nation. It is a book by a scholar and a wise American patriot who speaks from the heart about the nation he seeks to inspire to live its values and to achieve its full potential.

Henry Cisneros

ACKNOWLEDGMENTS

This is my fifth book. Mike Bieker, the director of the University of Arkansas Press, supported the project and offered me a contract. I was going to do the research during the summer in 2017, and then write it in the fall with the book going to press in 2018. It has been a tumultuous year. The nation has been in an existential crisis; Congress in gridlock, the nation polarized, and the Trump administration's immigration policies changing weekly. Having long supported thoughtful immigration reform, I was alarmed by the harshness of the policy changes, but thought undocumented youth were safe after Trump's campaign promises. I should have known better. I, like the undocumented youth and their supporters, was in limbo. With all the turmoil, I couldn't get my arms around the book project, so I abandoned it in August, thinking that my time could be better spent in other areas of the immigration reform movement. Then, on September 5, 2017, with the rescission of Deferred Action for Childhood Arrivals (DACA), I had pangs of guilt that I had abandoned the DACAmented whom I had known since they were teens. In early November, I attended the Blair Center Symposium on the Chicano movement, and as the audience was leaving the auditorium, Mike Bieker walked up and said, "Bill, you should write the book." I thought about it for a few days, talked about it with my wife, and a few days later called Mike and said I need to do something. I would like to write the book. Now that my work is at a close, I would like to acknowledge those people who aided me along the way.

First, thank you to Colette Brashears, Maria Cueva, Cali Deadman, Isamar Garcia-Hernandez, and Olivia Moore, students in my documentary film class, "DACA: The Arkansas Latino Experience." The class interviewed documented and undocumented youth, the DACAmented, administrators, professors, teachers, as well as those opposed to immigration reform. They videoed hours of interviews and their work provided the material for their documentary and research for this book.

Figure 0.1.
The DACAmented documented film students. From left to right: Colette Brashears, Olivia Moore, Maria Cueva, and Isamar Garcia-Hernandez (Cali Deadman missing from photo). Photograph by Zessna Garcia Rios.

We were the first class sponsored by The David and Barbara Pryor Center for Arkansas Oral and Visual History. We met at the center and their leadership and staff—Randy Dixon, Scott Lunsford, Dan Ferritor, Joshua Colvert, Susan Kendrick-Perry, and Sarah Moore—graciously shared their time, expertise, and space. Thanks also to Dean Todd Shields and Associate Dean Kathryn Sloan of the Fulbright College of Arts and Sciences for providing the class high-definition cameras, computers, editing software, and a budget for the project.

Thank you, also, to those interviewed for the book, especially Jeanette Arnhart, Laura Ferner, Mireya Reith, and Luis Restrepo. Your words place the plight of the undocumented into a legal, social, and political context. Once again, Zessna Garcia Rios and Juan Mendez, my deepest appreciation for coming out unafraid and sharing your lives with the readers. We have a better appreciation for the challenges Dreamers face because of you. Closer to campus, thank you to our campus Dreamers for sharing a coffee or a lunch to talk about all that was happening in your lives.

Susan Hall is an old and dear friend. She is my age and has been sitting in my classes for the past year. She has been a joy to me and my students and enriched our seminars. I told her that I needed fresh eyes on the manuscript, and she agreed to read it. Her editing and suggestions have made this a better book. Thank you, Susan.

A special thanks to Mike Bieker and the editorial and production staff at the University of Arkansas Press. I am always amazed at the amount of behind-the-scenes work involved in producing a book.

I could not have written this book without my wife, Judy. It's been a partnership. When I shared with her that I had talked to Mike and I needed to write the book, she supported my decision. Writing has always been difficult for me. That's why I have spent much of my life staring at the blank page. I think it is because I'm giving the reader a glimpse into my mind, and this is especially true when someone edits your work and must be critical of what you have created. It demands trust. Judy is a gifted writer and a former teacher of writing and over the past thirty-five years has helped me in my journey to become a better writer. Judy, your kindness, thoughtfulness, insights, and gentle hand made writing this book easier. As I have written before, I will always be your most grateful student. Voice, unity, coherence, and all the words of your craft now have meaning to me. Thank you for your passion for the written word and for your support these past thirty-five years. Not every author is as fortunate as I having a loving and supportive wife and friend.

A book is a collaborative enterprise. Peruse the notes, and you will find the researchers who contributed to this book. Thank you all for expanding our knowledge of the immigration process, the Dream movement, Deferred Action for Childhood Arrivals (DACA), and the experiences of undocumented youth. I have tried to faithfully represent your research and stories. If I have fallen short, I alone am responsible.

Introduction

When Mexico sends its people, they're not sending their best. They're not sending you. They're sending people that have lots of problems, and they're bringing those problems with us. They're bringing drugs. They're bringing crime. They're rapists. And some, I assume, are good people.

—DONALD TRUMP, PRESIDENTIAL ANNOUNCEMENT SPEECH, JUNE 16, 2015

In the 2016 campaign, Donald J. Trump offered a plan to "take back our country." He would expel eleven million immigrants and their families and let only "good people" back in. He would restrict legal immigration, impose a national job-verification system, and everyone would have to apply. He would build a two-thousand-mile border wall, which isn't needed, and make Mexico pay for it. He would replace the Constitution's guarantee of citizenship by birth with citizenship by fiat leaving it to politicians to decide. He would stop the reunification of immigrant families. And, he would flood the country with Immigration and Custom Enforcement (ICE) agents, create a climate of fear, and destroy America's standing as an immigrant-welcoming nation.

To the dismay of pollsters, pundits, and a majority of voters in the 2016 Presidential Election, this vision of America helped get him elected. In the opening days of his administration, Trump began implementing his vision. One of his first executive orders was a travel ban affecting seven predominantly Muslim countries. Within days, he directed the Department of Homeland Security to enhance border security, intensify ICE sweeps of immigrant neighborhoods, restrict the entry of already-sponsored refugees, and slash the number of visas vital to the nation's tourism, education, and high-technology sectors. A few weeks later, he included the border wall in his first budget. Then on September 5, 2017, he carried out his cruelest act and rescinded President Obama's executive order, Deferred Action for Childhood Arrivals (DACA), leaving in limbo hundreds of thousands of undocumented youth.

But does Trump have a mandate to implement these sweeping changes in our immigration policy? Are these policies ones that Americans embrace? The answer is *no*. A February 2017 Gallup Poll reported that nearly six-out-of ten Americans disapprove of the travel ban, construction of a border wall, and suspension of the refugee program. Gallup polls spanning a decade show that the majority of Americans, regardless of political party, support immigration, think immigration is good for the nation, and support a program that would allow undocumented youth to remain in the country and become citizens if they meet certain requirements. A meager 31 percent of Republican voters support Trump's policies on undocumented youth—a majority of Republicans favor a path to citizenship.

This disconnect between political rhetoric and public opinion is already surfacing. Federal courts have blocked the implementation of Trump's travel bans, governors are pushing back on visa restrictions, mayors are refusing to allow their police departments to participate in ICE sweeps because they destroy the trust between local governments and the immigrant communities they serve, and in January 2018 a federal district court judge reinstated DACA. There also has been an unprecedented mobilization of people and money to fight these policies because the American story is one of immigration. Unless you are Native American, you are an immigrant or are a descendent of an immigrant, and Americans celebrate their ancestry. Woven into the personal biographies of most of us are the hopes of millions of people who have journeyed here from abroad in search of opportunities. It is in the DNA of the American Dream where immigrants and native-born alike look for and believe in a better life for our children and ourselves. This history is why the majority of Americans embrace sensible immigration reform and oppose Trump's misanthropic policies.

It was a similar political climate in 2012 that motivated me to write

Right to DREAM: Immigration Reform and America's Future. I had completed a year-long study of the Hispanic community in Northwest Arkansas and had worked with undocumented students for years as professor and as dean. I studied the growth of my region's immigrant communities firsthand and was troubled by local police departments partnering with ICE to enforce federal laws. I was disturbed that we were creating a climate where skin color was probable cause for a traffic stop or a raid on a home, workplace, or apartment. I was outraged that we were deporting parents, forcing them to leave their US-born children behind to be raised by friends, siblings, or other relatives. As a community sociologist, it was unsettling to watch the creation of a permanent underclass, doing the "immigrant jobs" that no one else would do and, in the process, condemning our newest residents to the margins of our society. But for me, most disturbing were the lies of those opposed to immigration reform. I asked myself, "What contribution can I make to this debate?" My answer was I could write a book that would answer the critics by bringing a century of social science research on immigration to a general adult reading public.

Right to DREAM explored the critical issues facing the nation in shaping comprehensive immigration reform. What are the issues that divide? What did the proponents and opponents of immigration reform argue? Is there a middle ground? Is compromise possible? In answering these questions, I explained to my readers the legal issues surrounding immigration, who immigrants are, and why and how immigration has shaped this country, the effects of immigration on our economy and culture, and the process of becoming an American. I shared the stories of undocumented youth with whom I had worked. I described the DREAM Act that would have given undocumented youth legal status with a path to citizenship, and Deferred Action for Childhood Arrivals (DACA) an administrative action by the Obama administration that gave undocumented youth protected status. Since the Obama administration launched DACA in 2012, the US Citizenship and Immigration Services (USCIS) has approved nearly eight hundred thousand young people and denied only 1 percent of the applicants. While DACA did not offer a pathway to citizenship, it moved large numbers of eligible youth and young adults out of the shadows and into the mainstream of our society. And there is general agreement that the DACA program has been a wide-ranging success, integrating young adult immigrants into society and providing them economic opportunities that were previously unavailable. A national survey of undocumented Millennials showed that 70 percent say they began their first job or moved to a new job after receiving DACA, 64 percent say they are less afraid because of their status, and 84 percent now have a driver's license.

But the world changed on January 20, 2017, the day Donald J. Trump was inaugurated. Immigrant youth from around the country became afraid of being detained and deported under his new immigration policies. They were right to be alarmed. In January, he signed an executive order that ended the Obama administration's practice of focusing solely on violent offenders for deportation. Within days, ICE deported a mother of two US citizens who had lived in Phoenix for twenty years. Many young people fear that those who had Deferred Action for Childhood Arrivals are next.

I have worked with undocumented youth for a decade. I interviewed and collected more than fifty of their biographies for *Right to DREAM*, and I have kept in contact with many of them. I've talked to dozens of undocumented and DACAmented youth since November 2016, and they are alarmed. One experience that shaped my decision to write this book was a visit by the custodial worker in my building. I had gotten to know Mayra well. We talked almost every day, and I gave her a copy of my book. She and her husband are DACA recipients. Their Mexican parents brought them to Northwest Arkansas when they were children. As a result of DACA, Mayra and her husband have work permits—she works as a custodian, her husband works in construction. The jobs provide health insurance and other benefits for their family. They pay local, state, and federal taxes, and contribute to Social Security and Medicare, although they are ineligible for benefits. They have three children—an eleven-year-old son, and girls, ages four and five—all US citizens. They own a small house and two cars and have created a good life for their family in a stable neighborhood surrounded by a network of family and friends. They are pursuing the American Dream.

Mayra came in the day after the election and asked me, "What do you think will happen?" I told her I didn't know, but thought Trump's campaign rhetoric was one thing, governance another. She slumped into an office chair and through her tears said, "I have no memory of Mexico. I have little family left there. They are here. My children are Americans. They don't speak Spanish very well." She was terrified of being deported and leaving her children behind. Her sadness, depression, and loss were palpable. That day I asked myself, "What contribution can I make to this debate? I have to do something." I thought writing a book about the Mayras in this world could help—a book that would complement *Right to DREAM*. The title was obvious, *Dreams Derailed: Undocumented Youth in the Trump Era*.

Doing something is the goal of my book. I have written this book to help you make better informed decisions on the pivotal issues facing the nation on immigration. The book is organized around seven chapters.

Chapter 1, "The Rise of Trump and a Climate of Fear" explores the underlying political, demographic, and economic forces that shaped the 2016 presidential election and will shape elections to come. What are the forces that have contributed to the disturbing rise in the nation's inequality? Who are the winners and losers? Who has been left behind? American society is in the midst of the Fourth Wave of Immigration. How has it changed this society? When will white Americans become a minority? How has this fueled their resentment? What is the American Dream? Why do many Americans no longer believe in it? What are the consequences for this society when people think the system is rigged?

Chapter 2, "If Truth Be Told: Facts on Today's Immigration," counters the rise of alternative facts, fake news, and the art of lying. Presented in a question and answer format, the chapter explores some of the most egregious misinformation about immigration and the immigrants who live in our midst. For example, Trump opened his campaign saying, "Millions of illegal Mexicans cross our border each year." Truth: Since the Great Recession, more people are returning to Mexico than coming to the United States. Mexican migration is at a fifty-year low! The majority of the undocumented crossing our southern border are from Central America (many are children), and with enhanced border security, their numbers are dropping.

Chapter 3, "The Nation's Immigration Law: The DREAM Act (Development, Relief, and Education for Alien Minors Act) and DACA (Deferred Action for Childhood Arrivals) examines the nation's immigration and naturalization laws. Most Americans are unaware that the Obama administration implemented sweeping changes in our immigration policies through executive orders. Although the Obama administration deported a record number of undocumented people, it targeted felons, and DACA protected eight hundred thousand undocumented youth. Although the Trump administration's immigration policies are evolving, executive orders in the first one hundred days of his presidency have dismantled much of this policy. Presidential appointments to the Justice Department and Homeland Security suggest harsh and unforgiving enforcement. In this climate, what are the risks to DACA recipients and undocumented youth?

Chapter 4, "DACA by the Numbers: A Successful Policy, a Costly End" describes the success of the DACA program. Social scientists have tracked DACA recipients since the inception of the program, documenting the program's success. Of the nation's 1.9 million undocumented youth, eight hundred thousand participated in the program. They have Social Security cards and work permits and have entered the workforce. Since most are in their late teens, twenties, and early thirties, they are marrying and having children who are citizens. This chapter describes their economic and educational success, improvements in their psychological well being, their impact on neighborhoods and communities, and the benefits to our nation as we tap our investments in these young people. It also answers questions about the DACAmented. How many were eligible for DACA and how many received relief? Who are they? Where do they live? What are they doing? How are they doing? Are they integrating into the fabric of our communities and society? And, what are the costs of ending the program?

Chapter 5, "Allies: Four People Making a Difference" describes the fight for a just and inclusive immigration system that cannot happen without advocates and allies of the DACAmented. We learn of the contributions of four of them who are quietly working in the background, investing their time, money, and careers in bringing about social change.

In chapter 6, "Old Friends: Zessna Garcia and Juan Mendez," I revisit Garcia and Mendez, two Dreamers profiled in *Right to DREAM*. Readers will discover the remarkable contributions these young people have made to their communities since receiving deferred action. Learn of their lives before and after they were awarded deferred action protections. Where are they from? What challenges did they face growing up here? What are their hopes and fears since the November election? Now that DACA has been repealed, what will they do? How will they cope? How will they fight back? Will they be forced from their careers into an underground economy in a nation desperate for their talents? What are their hopes for a future?

Chapter 7, "Next Steps: Where We Go from Here," revisits our recent past and looks ahead. This time is one of great uncertainty. In the 2016 elections, Republicans took the White House and both houses of Congress by appealing to the fears and nationalistic instincts of the electorate. We will take a long and short view of this social change. The long view of social change is that there are two profound demographic changes reshaping our nation—the first is generational and the second is ethnic and racial. In 2019, the Millennials will outnumber the Baby Boomers, and by midcentury there will not be a racial or ethnic majority in this society. Will demographic change affect political change? The short view is throughout our history, social movements have reshaped this society. There is strong evidence that once again these movements are changing social norms, gun control legislation, and immigration policy. The book ends urging next steps.

Nations have the sovereign right to control their borders and decide whom they wish to enter their society. Immigration policy shapes our national identity and determines what it means to be an American. This is why it is such an emotional issue. The question lingers: Will our long history of welcoming immigrants continue, will it change our national character, and what is the future of immigration in the United States? Immigration is a complex and fascinating subject; our past determines the present and shapes our future. We begin by exploring the social, economic, demographic, and cultural forces that brought Donald J. Trump to the White House.

Dreams Derailed

ONE

The Rise of Trump and a Climate of Fear

I texted and e-mailed my friends the morning after the 2016 presidential election, but no one replied. They, like the majority of the nation, were stunned by the previous night's results. When I made my way to campus that morning, I began to hear that some young, white males—apparently emboldened by the election—were assailing students of color. Their message of "white power" was clear and intimidating: "You are no longer welcome on this campus. Get out. Go home."

The university had spent decades reaching out to underrepresented students in the state—and in particular to African American students in the Arkansas Delta and Hispanic students in Northwest Arkansas. In the days and weeks ahead, many faculty, staff, and students—including some who had voted for Donald Trump—became anxious, if not fearful, that a small cohort could reverse the institution's trajectory toward inclusion and intercultural understanding. What is more disturbing, however, is that the message of white power and intolerance has reverberated at campuses and communities across the country.

Issues like race, class, and inequality seem as polarizing today as they were in the 1960s. Political norms are imploding, and the very notion of civil discourse is being sorely tested. Americans are unfriending one another on Facebook, ending decades-long friendships, avoiding one another at the grocery store, and approaching family gatherings with caution. Conversational minefields abound. There is very little safe ground, with the exception of children and grandchildren.

In fact, many historians believe that our nation is as divided today as we were on the eve of the Civil War. Fault lines in our society have grown deeper between urban and rural populations; among people of color—black, brown, and white; between citizens and immigrants; among the geographical divides of the Northeast and the West and the South and the Midwest; and, of course, between Democrats and Republicans. The result? We are in the midst of a cold civil war.

Of all the issues that divide Americans today, immigration may be the best example of the existential crisis in which we find ourselves. The very word provokes core questions, such as: Who are we? What are our values? How have the forty-three million immigrants and their forty million children changed us? How do we treat these strangers in our midst? What does it mean to be an American? If we cannot trace our ancestry to Native Americans, are we, too, immigrants?

The pundits have had a year to dissect Trump's victory—a victory that caught them as off guard as it did the general public. They've pointed to Hillary Clinton's lackluster campaigning; her framing of issues around inclusion, LBGTQ rights, and the plight of the undocumented; and her demonizing potential working-class voters as "deplorables." Some critics point to the legacy of her husband—for better and for worse. Others talk about the challenges women still face in politics and business and beyond.

Their emerging consensus is that Donald J. Trump was the only primary or general election candidate who understood the simmering resentment of fifty million, overwhelmingly white, Americans who feel left behind by our society—voters all but forgotten by both major political parties. And his rhetoric—"Drain the swamp!" "Lock her up!" "Build the wall!"—resonated with them.

We tend to live in the present. We look for proximate causes. However, the election and the surge of anti-immigration sentiment happened because of changes at work in American society for a half century. In this chapter, we will explore the "why" by examining three profound societal changes that laid the foundation for the rise and election of Trump.

First, globalization: the ascent of an information and knowledge-based economy and growing inequality. The winners and losers in this new economy now define our body politic.

Second, the nation's Fourth Wave of Immigration. Today, one of every four people living in the United States is a first- or second-generation immigrant. We have not seen numbers like these in a century. The growth in this figure, especially the eleven million undocumented ones, when combined with the realization that within a generation the majority of us will be from minority groups—black, Asian, and Hispanic—furthers white resentment. Some exit polls in the 2016 election showed that many voters voted against their economic self-interest in favor of their cultural one.[1]

Finally, the loss of faith in the American Dream. The American Dream has always included belief in the freedom to choose the direction of one's life; confidence that one's knowledge, skills, and abilities will be recognized and rewarded; trust that one's children will be better off than preceding generations; and faith in a brighter future. Opinion polls show that many Americans no longer share these beliefs. Instead they feel that a rigged system has excluded them from the American Dream, and they have been left behind.

Globalization: Social Trends and Political Consequences

Donald Trump and Hillary Clinton presented starkly different images of America. Clinton envisioned a society of inclusion, an economy that served all, and strength through diversity. She called those who injected racism, homophobia, and sexism into the campaign, *deplorables*. Trump, in contrast, pictured a rigged political and economic system that served the few and created working-class victims. And he called the beneficiaries of this unfair system *majority-minority line jumpers*. Clinton won the popular vote; Trump won the Electoral College and the presidency. So, what were the themes in Trump's campaign that resonated? First and most important was "Make America Great Again"—the idea that his economic policies would stop the off-shoring of jobs and create good-paying manufacturing jobs. Second, he promised he would "Build the Wall" to stop illegal immigration, sharply curtail visas, and protect American workers. Finally, he promised a renewal of the American Dream.

Make America Great Again

This message is economic populism, but does this frame the economy accurately? Will nationalist policies revive manufacturing and bring good-paying jobs home? Most economists think not. They point to changes brought about by globalization, the types of the jobs needed in our new economy, and the regions where firms are creating them. The truth is the rise of a global, knowledge- and information-based economy is at the root of these problems.[2] The core question is: "How did this revolution come about?" The answer is that four profound, independent social and technological changes converged in the 1980s making the globalization of the world economy possible. They were the democratization of technology, finance, information, and decision making, along with a change in the global political order resulting from the fall of the Berlin Wall and the collapse of the Soviet Union. Many social scientists view globalization and the emergence of a post-industrial society as a revolution as profound in human history as the Agricultural and the Industrial revolutions.[3]

The Democratization of Technology

In today's global market economy, a company can build anything virtually anyplace in the world. Innovations in computers, telecommunications, digitization, and automation allow billions of people in the world to be connected and to exchange information and knowledge. With the democratization of technology, most countries now have the technology to produce highly finished goods. If a nation has a core of well-educated and highly skilled workers, it can import the technology it needs. Sourcing funds from investors in one nation, subcontractors of components in another, shippers, accountants, and marketers in still others has been commonplace. These new relationships span the globe and are made possible by the master technology—the Internet.

Examples of the democratization of technology are endless, but the smartphone in your pocket or purse is a good one. Apple manages a supply chain of more than two hundred vendors in different countries and continents and then funnels these parts into a single device assembled in China. Companies around the globe make the screens and touch ID sensors, cameras, processors, and memory cards. Probably the only American who touches your phone is the FedEx driver who delivers it to your home. Yet Apple—headquartered in Cupertino, California—makes most of the profit because it does the high value-added design, programing, and marketing. This change in technology has given corporations, like Apple, an enormous advantage in scouring the world for the lowest costs of essential inputs—raw materials, components, labor, investment, and facilities. Why not manufacture domestically? High labor costs in the United States give other countries a clear advantage.

The Democratization of Finance

Before the 1980s, most business lending was controlled by New York's commercial banks. In the 1980s, laws changed, and new actors entered financial markets using a dizzying array of new financial instruments to raise investment capital. These funds finance every conceivable activity in the global economy, and groups who have never before had access to capital now have a global financial market to tap using the Internet. Because of these changes, during the first decades of globalization, more wealth has been created in a shorter period than at any other time in human history. The 2003 and 2008 financial crises exposed the downside of global markets—homeowners and investors lost trillions of dollars.

The Democratization of Information

The democratization of information was made possible by the digitization of data, high-speed computers, electronic data storage, and the Internet. With a computer and a high-speed Internet connection, anyone can access information and knowledge anyplace in the world. And Google, Amazon, Siri, and Alexa have become indispensable parts of our lives. This change is essential in other ways. How do you know where to invest your capital for the highest return at the lowest risk? Without the Internet and the democratization of information, the global economy would be impossible. This development is the third piece of the globalization puzzle.

The Democratization of Decision Making

Before globalization, most decisions made by government or corporations occurred from the top down and at a snail's pace. Not anymore. Because of the democratization of technology, the person at the top is quickly overwhelmed by information. As a result, the role of top managers has changed. Corporate executives no longer make the day-to-day decisions they once did; they are paid to develop strategies and to broker deals. Other decisions have been decentralized to people with the technical expertise to make them. The same is true for nations. Information is power, and with the decentralization of decision making, citizens have at their fingertips information once hidden in the bowels of the bureaucracy. Nothing is more effective at keeping elected officials honest than knowing someone is looking over their shoulder. Scandals often bring reform and stability to a political system and greater predictability and stability to the global economy. This is the democratization of decision-making's contribution to globalization.

Therefore, changes in technology, finance, information, and decision making have made the global economy possible. They have lowered the costs of entering a market, empowered consumers, shortened the product cycle, and kept prices low, ultimately unleashing the power of capitalism to create new products and wealth. Today, a nation's most important assets are the skills and talents of its people; and the global, not national, economy determines their incomes based on their contributions to the value of goods and services sold in the global marketplace.

But there are winners and losers in the new economy. Those who have the skills to navigate the global economy are rewarded with ever-greater income and wealth while the less skilled are consigned to a declining standard of living. Consequently, most of the growth in our economy has gone to the top one or two percent and, as a result, we now have the greatest income and wealth inequality in our nation's history, levels not seen since the Gilded Age.

The 2016 election exposed the strains that this inequality has created in our political and social fabric. So, who are the winners and losers in the new economy? Most of our workforce falls into four categories: routine production workers, in-person service workers, symbolic analysts, and place-bound professions—with each group having a different trajectory.[4]

Routine Production Services

Routine production services are blue-collar factory and entry-level clerical workers. Their work is repetitive and requires a less sophisticated skill set. Their employers typically pay by the hour. These jobs remain in high demand in the global economy as we still need cars, appliances, and computers assembled, data entered, and reports filed, but these workers are vulnerable because a world market determines the value of their work. Data entry, for example, can be done as well and more cheaply, via the Internet, in India or thousands of other places in the world besides the United States.

Table 1.1. Jobs in the Twenty-First Century Economy

Type	Replaceable	Outsourcing	Future?
Routine Production Workers	Yes	Yes	Downward
In-Person Service Workers	Yes	Some	Slowly downward
Symbolic-Analytic Workers	No	Some	Growing
Place-Bound Professionals	No	No	Stable

Source: This table was developed from chapter 2, "Globalization and Urbanization in the More-Developed World" in my book, *Deciphering the City* (Upper Saddle River, NJ: Prentice Hall, 2005).

In-Person Services

As with routine production services, in-person services tend to be repetitive and require less specialized skill sets and only a high school education. They include telephone operators, airline reservationists, retail clerks, waiters, janitors, telemarketers, hospital and nursing home workers, and workers in the hospitality industry. Like routine production workers, they are paid by the hour. Since they provide their services in-person, employers can't outsource them. Most service workers make minimum wage. This category of workers is one of the fastest growing in the nation, and they make up approximately 30 percent of our workforce.

Symbolic-Analytic Services

Symbolic-analytic services is the third job category. They require a skill set that includes problem solving, problem identifying, and strategic brokering. These workers compete for jobs in a global economy, but they do not do routine, standardized tasks. Traded instead are their skills, talents, and intellectual property. They are not paid by the hour or for the amount of work they do, but by the value they add to the things they help produce. They are engineers, bankers, lawyers, developers, and those involved in the financial services industry. Symbolic analysts solve, identify, and broker problems by manipulating symbols, not things. Most symbolic analysts have college degrees, and unlike the other two categories, experience counts. Symbolic analysts hone their skills by doing, and the value of these workers increases over time. They make up approximately 20 percent of the American workforce.

Place-Bound Professions

Place-bound professionals are the doctors, dentists, teachers, professors, administrators, police, firemen, health professionals, and an array of highly skilled workers who keep our bodies, homes, offices, and factories working. Most of them have technical, college, or professional degrees. Since they provide their services locally and in person, they have little competition in the global economy.

Three factors shape the future of each of these groups: first, their replaceability; second, the value they add to a product or service; and third, the value their goods and services bring in the global economy. The future of the routine service worker is bleak. The reality is that employers can easily replace them, they add little to the value of a product, and their work can be done by a worker in China or India for a fraction of the cost in the United States. Routine labor costs around the world determine their future. The majority of these workers voted for Trump. These were the voters who responded to his message, "What do you have to lose?"

You might think in-person-service workers would be safe, but are they? Since they provide their services in person, you wouldn't think employers could easily replace them. Although they offer services in person, they typically don't add a great deal of value to a product. Does this mean, however, that firms can't replace them? When was the last time you stepped inside a bank? Banks have slashed their workforce by substituting ATMs and on-line banking. Computers have replaced telephone operators. We make most of our airline and hotel reservations on sites like Expedia and Travelocity. The future of those who work in retail? Think Amazon. Service workers will experience downward social mobility.

Corporations are outsourcing some of the work of symbolic analysts, but most have a rosy future. Employers can't easily replace them. In some cases, they hold the fate of a firm in their hands. Their skills are in high demand, and their value increases with experience. Their skills are bought and sold in a global economy, but unlike the other two groups, their skills are in short supply, and high demand means high incomes. Symbolic analysts give higher value to products, and they are in a position to demand a higher standard of living. In the twenty-first century, most of the wealth created in the world will go to this group. Similarly, place-bound professionals have a bright future because they are highly skilled and can't be easily replaced or outsourced.

The cities and states where these jobs are being created and lost is another essential part of the story. Symbolic analysts thrive in collaborative groups, and more and more these groups are found in innovation centers on the East and West coasts, the Chicago metro complex, and the Dallas-Austin-Houston corridor. Here one finds the most

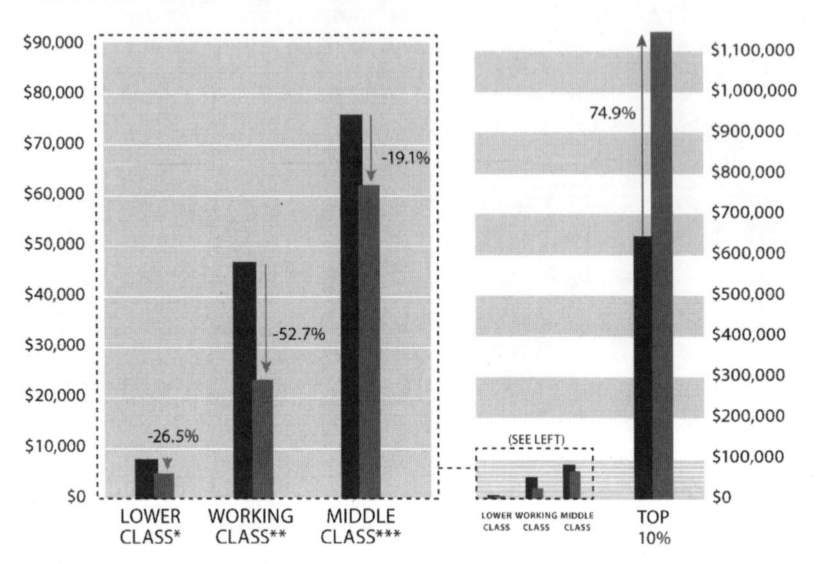

Figure 1.1.
The Wealth Inequality Problem in One Chart
It's Clear that America's Financial and Political Systems are Broken.

Courtesy of the Federal Reserve Survey of Consumer Finances; figures in 2013 dollars. *Bottom 20% of incomes; **second lowest 20% of incomes; ***middle 20% of incomes.

productive, creative, and best-paid workers in the nation, and cities with prosperous economies based in the new economy. At the other end of the continuum are manufacturing cities with an economy based on the old economy. Typically found in the Rust Belt and Heartland, these centers are losing jobs and residents. Thus, the geography of jobs reflects the economic changes wrought by globalization, and as we saw in the 2016 election, the blue states were on the coasts and red states in the interior—one region prospering, the other distressed.[5]

The consequence of these trajectories is a rising standard of living for the educated and skilled and a decline for the others in our economy. And there is overwhelming evidence that it has already occurred. Income is money coming into a family, while wealth is a family's assets. In the opening decades of the twenty-first century, most of the nation's wealth and income growth have gone to the top 1 percent with modest growth to the top 20 percent. (See figure 1.1).

In November 2017 the Pew Research Center, a nonpartisan Washington, D.C.-based think tank, reported that the "wealth gaps between upper-income families and lower- and middle-income families are at the highest levels ever recorded. . . . In 2016, the median wealth of lower-income families was 42 percent less than in 2007, and the median wealth of middle-income families was 33 percent lower." In sharp contrast, "The median wealth of upper-income families is at the highest level since the Federal Reserve started collecting these data in 1983." Income figures show the same pattern. Income inequality in the United States, on the rise for decades, is now the highest since 1928.[6] Across groups, the gaps between rich and poor and between whites and minorities have grown wider in recent years.[7]

But have manufacturing jobs left the United States in the hundreds of thousands because of bad trade deals such as NAFTA and since China joined the World Trade Organization? The answer is no. The United States did lose almost six million manufacturing jobs between 2000–2010, but according to a study by the Center for Business and Economic Research at Ball State University, 85 percent of these job losses are attributable to automation rather than international trade. Automation has transformed American manufacturing, but at a cost—the loss of millions of low-skilled, middle-income jobs. Figure 1.2 shows we produce more than twice as much as a generation ago but with fewer people because US factories are gradually replacing workers with robots. The math is simple. A welder earns around $25 an hour with benefits; a robot does the same work for $8 an hour, and without benefits.[8]

Tragically, the new factories have left behind millions of poorly educated, low-skilled, and primarily white workers. J. D. Vance vividly portrays their plight in his *New York Times* bestseller, *Hillbilly Elegy: A Memoir of a Family and Culture in Crisis*. Vance offers a compassionate, astute sociological analysis of the white underclass that drove the politics that elected Donald Trump. Set in Middletown, Ohio, a Rust Belt city in the midst of a painful transition to the new economy, he describes the economic insecurity and psychological hazards of people

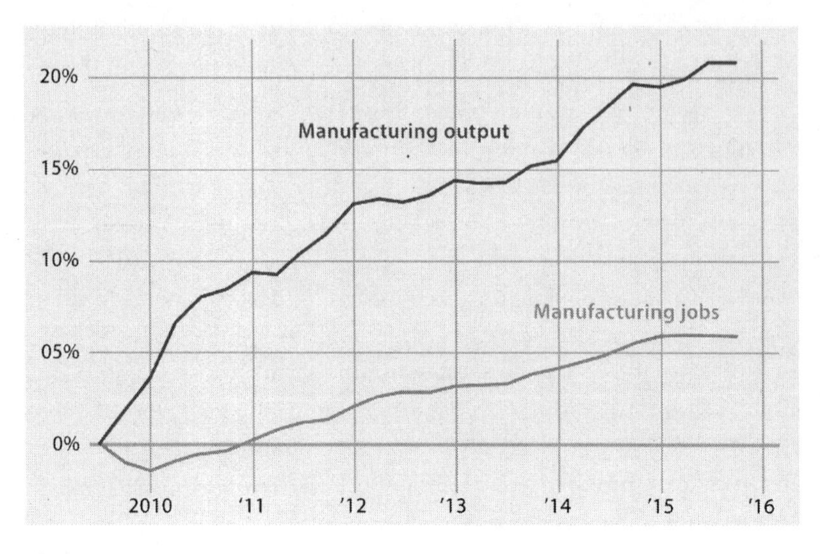

Figure 1.2

A Renaissance in Production, Not Jobs. Manufacturing Production vs. Employment, Percentage Change Since the End of the Most Recent Recession. Courtesy of the Federal Reserve, Bureau of Labor Statistics.

caught in an economy where they are not needed, where for them there are only minimum-wage jobs at best and unemployment at worst. For the most part, they live lives of despair.

Social scientists have developed an "Index of Despair" to measure and describe the levels of despair. Opiate deaths are a good proxy, and map 1.1 shows their distribution. Note the death rates peak along a broadband from Appalachia through the Ozarks to Oklahoma, much of it crossing the nation's manufacturing heartland. Nationally, the new economy has left more than fifty million Americans behind, and their anger over an economic system that left them on the margins of our society helped decide the 2016 election.

As I have shown, the forces of globalization have fundamentally changed our economy and the nature of work, producing winners and losers. But there is an equally important source of anger and despair, and that is the changing demographic character of our society.

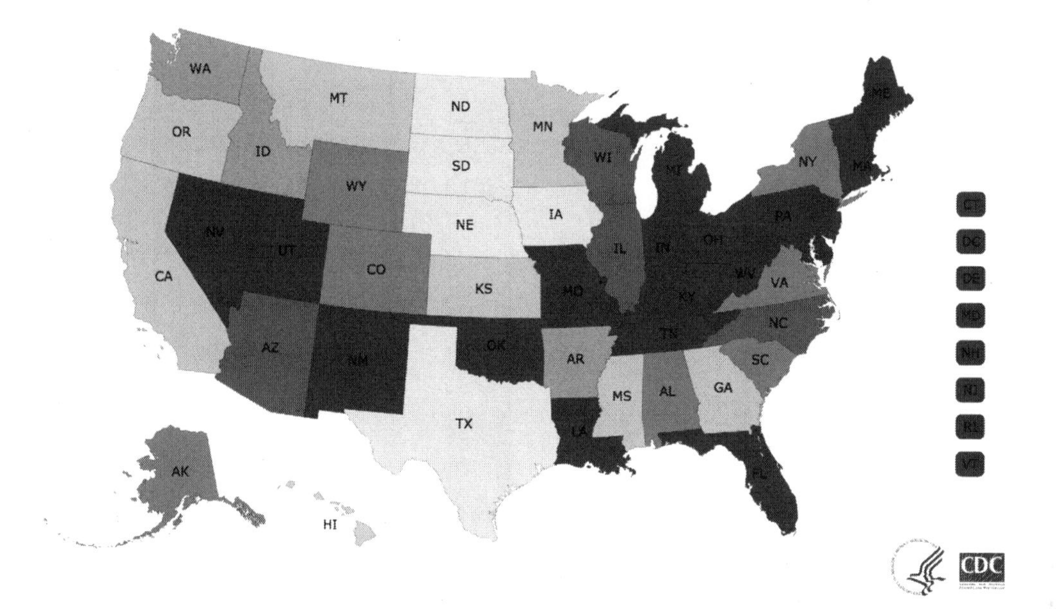

Map 1.1

The Nation's Opiate Deaths

Sources: Park, H., and M. Block. 2016. "How the Epidemic of Drug Overdose Deaths Rippled across America," https://www.nytimes.com/interactive/2016/01/07/us/drug-overdose-deaths-in-the-us.html, accessed November 21, 2017; Rossen, Lauren M., Brigham Bastian, Margaret Warner, Diba Khan, and Yinong Chong. "Drug Poisoning Mortality in the United States, 1994–2015." National Center for Health Statistics, Centers for Disease Control and Prevention, accessed November 21, 2017.

Immigration

In 2015, the United States naturalized 730,259 people. The leading countries of birth were Mexico, India, the Philippines, and the People's Republic of China.[9] That same year United States Citizenship and Immigration Services granted permanent legal residency to 1.1 million immigrants with more than two hundred nationalities.[10] Now, as in our past, no nation in history has accepted as its citizens, albeit sometimes reluctantly, a more diverse populace than the United States. On the one hand, it is one of the nation's strengths: we have brought together the talents and the perspectives of many cultures in defining our national character. On the other hand, immigration has been a source of great division at times creating cleavages that weakened our political and

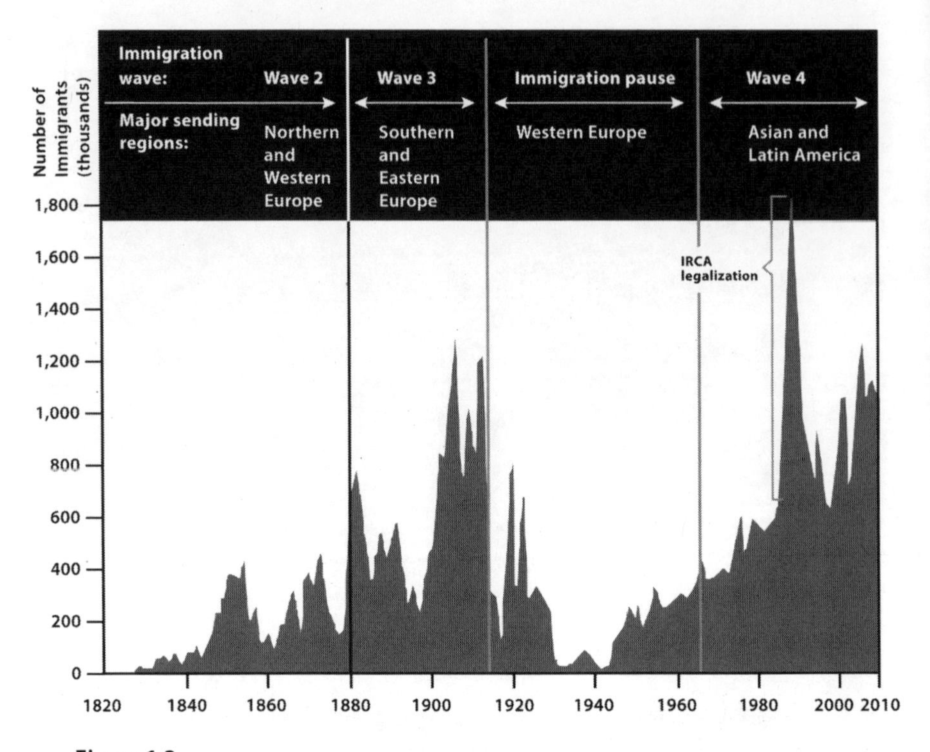

Figure 1.3

America's Four Waves of Immigration: 1820–2010 US.

Source: Census Bureau, Census of Population and Housing and Department of Homeland Security see also: The US and World's Immigration Visualized in two maps; http://metrocosm.com/animated-immigration-map/; http://metrocosm.com/global-immigration-map/, accessed June 11, 2012.

social fabric. The miracle of this nation is that such a diverse community of peoples can live together in peace.

The twentieth century witnessed the transformation of the United States from a predominately white population rooted in Western culture to a society with an array of racial, ethnic, and religious minorities. At the beginning of the twentieth century, the US population was 87 percent white. The nonwhite minority was composed primarily of African Americans living in the rural South. In the second decade of the twenty-first century, whites still account for 72 percent of the US population, but a profound demographic shift is underway. In 2014, the Census Bureau reported that for the first time in our history, more minority children (African American, Hispanic, and Asian American) than white children were enrolled in our public schools.[11] Americans now realize that within twenty years, the majority of Americans will be minority, and the United States will have become a majority-minority society.[12] This is a source of white resentment.

I recently overheard this conversation with a Tea Party member. She was born in Mountain Home, Arkansas, in the early 1940s and married and raised her family in Little Rock. She and her husband returned to Northwest Arkansas when they retired. She had many grievances, but the one that stayed with me most was, "I'm going to die in a country I no longer recognize." She was born in a society that was overwhelming white; she will die in a society where she will be in the minority.

We have a long history of immigration, and our past shows that we have grown and prospered by it. At the beginning of the twentieth century, many Americans were concerned about the growing number of immigrants from Eastern, Central, and Southern Europe, and industrialization and urbanization were the forces transforming our nation and its economy. At the beginning of the twenty-first century, immigration is again a concern of Americans, but this time the immigrants are from Latin America and Asia, and globalization is transforming the nation and its economy.[13]

Another theme in the Trump Campaign was the promise to "Build the Wall" along the Mexican border to stop illegal immigration, sharply curtail visas, and protect American workers. And the reason this message resonated was the visibility of the Fourth Wave. If you combine the forty-three million immigrants living in our nation with the forty million children who have at least one foreign-born parent, then one of every four people living here is a first- or second-generation immigrant. We have not seen these numbers since the opening decades of the twentieth century. And don't forget about the eleven million unauthorized immigrants living in our midst. They have become the touchstone for the anti-immigrant forces in our society and a major theme in the Clinton and Trump campaigns. Clinton's solution was to provide a path to citizenship; Trump's was to deport them.

There is still another factor. Immigrants historically have entered through gateways like New York, San Francisco, Los Angeles, Miami,

Dallas, and Houston; but many immigrants in this new wave have settled in states like Arkansas, Alabama, Mississippi, North Carolina, Kansas, and Nebraska—the deep South and the Heartland. Cities like Chicago, St. Louis, Kansas City, and Denver have absorbed millions of new residents, too. These states and cities have not experienced mass immigration in more than a century, and this is where we encounter the most hostility to immigration. Demographic change reinforced changes wrought by the new economy, and the tensions in our communities shook our political system. Immigration is the second part of the Trump story.

The American Dream

There are three elements of the American Dream: the freedom to pursue happiness, the promise of economic security, and optimism for the future.[14] For the majority of Americans, the last decade was a "lost decade" with flat and declining wages, with middle-class jobs disappearing—seeming never to reappear—after the Great Recession. In 2017 median incomes are only now reaching prerecession levels. To what degree have Americans continued to believe in the American Dream?

Surveys continue to show that large numbers of Americans still believe in many of the ideals of the American Dream, but a recent McClatchy-Marist Poll suggests their faith may be wavering.[15]

- Close to seven-in-ten Americans think people can work hard and still have difficulty maintaining their standard of living or not get ahead. Most say there are different rules for the well connected, and a majority of Americans believe government policies put the middle class at a disadvantage.
- Many Americans no longer think hard work translates into upward mobility. Sixty-eight percent think people who work hard in this country still have a difficult time maintaining their standard of living.
- Most Americans think the concept of a level-playing field is unrealistic. Eighty-five percent of adults think, when it comes to getting ahead, there are different rules for the well connected and the wealthy.

- More than three-in-four Americans don't believe the next generation will have it any easier. Seventy-eight percent say it will take more effort for them to advance.
- Fifty-five percent of adults across the nation think that the middle class, more than other socioeconomic groups, is being left behind by government policies. Four-in-ten believe the poor are being excluded while only 4 percent say the rich are being left out.
- Sixty percent of white Americans and 53 percent of Latinos think government policies shut out the middle class. However, nearly six-in-ten African Americans report that the poor are the ones who are excluded.

There is evidence that the scope of the American Dream is changing as well. Homeownership and upper mobility have long been equated with the American Dream, but middle-class Americans are changing their priorities. In 2015, the Pew Research Center asked its sample which they would prefer—financial security or moving up the income ladder—92 percent selected security.[16] And these economic and social changes have hit the Millennials the hardest. They are our largest generation, and they, more than any other generation, have abandoned the dream.[17] One of my former students summed it up for me. She told me, "My husband and I want kids, a house, and a retirement fund like everyone else, but on our salaries, we can only have two of the three."

Today, for most Americans, achieving the American Dream is just that, a dream, a downsized dream, and this change in our nation's psyche has social and political ramifications. When citizens are more concerned about moving down the socioeconomic ladder rather than moving up, there are grave consequences for our society. In 2016 voters looking for scapegoats and solutions turned to an unexpected savior, Donald J. Trump.

Closing the Circle

To this point, we have argued that we are in the midst of a revolution—a revolution that is creating a global economy made possible by the democratization of technology, finance, information, and decision making.

These changes lowered the barrier of entry into markets, empowered consumers, shortened the product cycle, and unleashed the creative power of people through free-market capitalism. The first decades of this revolution created more wealth than at any other time in history as well as enormous inequality.

In the United States, corporations have been transformed from national to global entities; the economy has shifted from high-volume to high-value-added production; and human capital has become the nation's most important asset. As part of the global economy we helped to create, the well being of our citizens has become tied to the value they add to products through their knowledge, skills, and abilities. This transformation created an unprecedented amount of national wealth in which not all Americans share. The nation's well educated and highly skilled have watched their standard of living soar, while most Americans, trapped at the margins of the revolution, have watched theirs stagnate or decline.

A demographic transformation has accompanied this economic one—one-quarter of the people living in the United States are first- or second-generation immigrants. These numbers have not been seen in nearly a century, and we know from our history that when large numbers of immigrants enter our society—especially when there are significant cultural differences—suspicion mounts, social angst swells, and political repercussions abound.

This nation has seen similar political upheaval before. Figure 1.4 superimposes two graphs—income inequality (top 10 percent) and immigrants' share of the US population. They closely track each other. First, note that inequality now exceeds the levels last visited during the Gilded Age, when the Rockefellers, Vanderbilts, Morgans, Duponts, and other families controlled much of the nation's wealth. They were able to profit from the unprecedented explosion of new industrial and agricultural technology that drove changes in the economy. For example, the Rockefellers profited from advances in technology related to oil; the Vanderbilts, railroads; J. P. Morgan, banking; and the Duponts, chemicals. Today, we have billionaires like Bill Gates, Jeff Bezos, and Mark Zuckerberg whose wealth comes from the creation of investments in new technologies—Gates founded Microsoft; Bezos, Amazon; and Zuckerberg, Facebook.

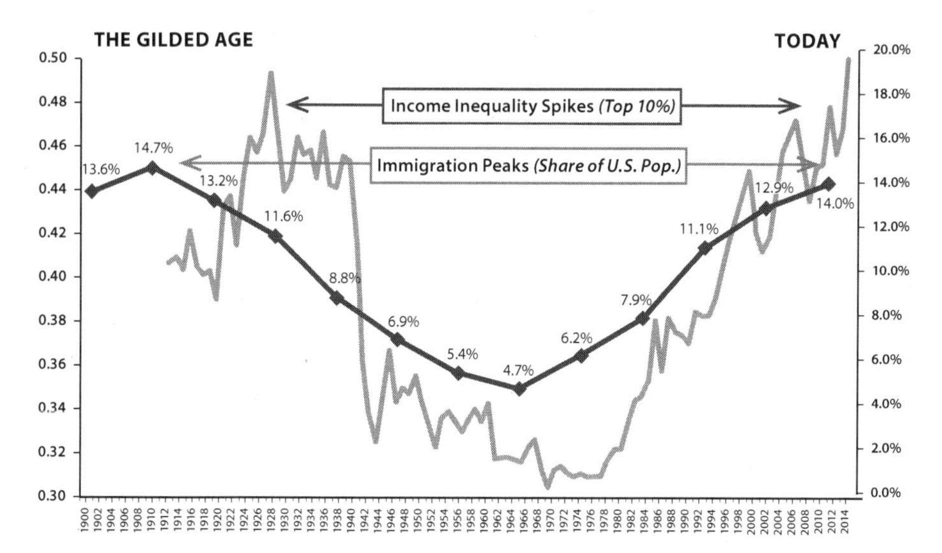

Figure 1.4

Demographic Disruptions Drive Social Angst

As Income Inequality Grew, Many in the "Bottom 90%" Blamed the Rapid Rise of Immigrants . . . Who No Longer Looked Like Them.

Source: Mehlman, B. 2017. "Navigating the New Gilded Age: Why Change Is Coming Again." http://mehlmancastagnetti.com/wp-content/uploads/Mehlman-New-Gilded-Age-Q4-2017.pdf, slide 7, accessed September 29, 2017.

Immigration was also a divisive issue during the Gilded Age, a time when America's metropolitan populations exploded. By 1900, America's thirty million city dwellers represented 40 percent of the US population, and half of these new urban residents were immigrants, the vast majority of whom were from Southern and Eastern Europe and Asia. These immigrants differed from the native-born population with its roots in Northern and Western Europe. During the 1880s, five million people immigrated to our shores. In the decade running up to the twentieth century, there were 3.7 million arrivals. In 1910, 14.7 percent of our population was foreign-born, and this growth strained our society and shaped our politics. Today, history repeats itself. Fourteen percent of our population is foreign born, and the source of new arrivals has once again shifted, this time to Latin America and Asia. And, as in the past, economic change and immigration shape our politics.

Although separated by nearly a century, the themes in our political

Figure 1.5

Fear and Frustration Fuel Populist Backlash.

Source: Mehlman, B. 2017. "Navigating the New Gilded Age: Why Change Is Coming Again," http://mehlmancastagnetti.com/wp-content/uploads/Mehlman-New-Gilded-Age-Q4-2017.pdf, slide 8, accessed September 29, 2017.

discourse today are remarkably similar to those of the Gilded Age.[18] And, as in our past there has been a populist backlash with similar themes: "Blame the Immigrants," "Fault Trade," "Hit Globalists," and "Attack the Parties." Sound familiar? (See figure 1.5.) A century ago it was rural to urban migration, rapid urbanization, industrialization, and mass immigration. Today, it is globalization, the rise of a knowledge- and information-based economy, and mass immigration. Donald J. Trump was elected because he was smart enough to tap into the fears and frustrations of millions of Americans whom the economy has left behind, who felt Hillary Clinton disparaged them, and whom immigration made feel like strangers in their own land.

A Profile

The pundits blew it; not one of them predicted the Trump victory, but a sociologist did, Arlie Russell Hochschild. Professor Hochschild is one of the nation's most respected ethnographers, and she had spent five years in the Saint Charles, Louisiana, region in the years before the 2016 election trying to understand the rise of the Tea Party. Her book, *Strangers in Their Own Land: Anger and Mourning of the American Right*, provides insight into the rise of Trump and his election. There are three themes in her book. First, empathy walls: Why can we no longer discuss politics and social problems? Second: Why the rise of the Tea Party? And, third, the Great Paradox: Why do people vote against their economic self-interest?

Empathy is "the ability to understand and share the feelings of another," and as a society, the racial, economic, and gender divide has always made it difficult to understand people different from us. Characteristics like race, class, gender, and sexual preference erect barriers, and our politics exacerbate them by exploiting issues like Confederate statues, violent gangs, welfare queens, and immigration for short-term political gain. It is a reinforcing cycle, and we can see these differences in our nation's geography. Innovation centers grow in states on the coasts and old-economy manufacturing in the ones in the interior. Coastal states are becoming more ethnically and racially diverse, the interior ones whiter. Our cities are becoming more segregated with income now more important than race in describing where people live. Maps of red and blue states vividly show this social divide—blue states on the coasts and upper Midwest and red states in the Old South and Heartland.

Maps of our cities show neighborhoods segregated by income, ethnicity, and race—separate and unequal. The lack of empathy is social, political, and spatial. People who are different seldom talk because we live in different social worlds where our neighbors, churches, schools, and media reinforce our values and beliefs—echo chambers where there are few disturbing words. This isolation from diverse perspectives contributes to the decline in empathetic, civil, civic debate, and destruction of the norms that have historically guided these discussions.

I found Arlie Hochschild's analysis of the Tea Party valuable in lowering my empathy wall. I, like many Americans, didn't understand what made the Tea Party tick. Here is what Hochschild found. The Tea Party agenda maintains distrust of big government, conviction of a rigged system, animosity toward taxes thought to be too high and too progressive, rejection of government aid, devaluation of religious and personal values, dishonor due to misrepresentation in the media, and a belief that immigrants and minorities are line jumpers—all of which lead to a strong sense of alienation and defiance. Horschild's research also uncovered five types of Tea Party members. The *American Dream Lost* members feel left behind by a changing economy. The *Line Cutter* members believe minorities, women, federal workers, and immigrants are getting ahead because of government policy and not merit. The *Betrayed* members believe that our society no longer works for them and they feel ignored and demeaned. The *Downsized* members have watched low-skilled, middle-income jobs disappear with only low-wage employment remaining. And *Catcall* members are white, working-class Christians who feel their values and beliefs are mocked by society, and feel the honor of their class is fading along with their population.

The three themes developed in this chapter explain their ideology and the rise of Trump. They are the millions of Americans who find themselves in a perilous economic group—American Dream Lost. They are the groups most affected by a majority-minority society—"Build the Wall" mentality. And they are the ones marginalized by their views on abortion, gender roles, gay rights, race, immigration, and guns—"Make America Great Again."

And here is the Great Paradox—these groups vote for candidates endorsed by the Tea Party who have positions that are not in their economic self-interest. They may hate government and taxes, but they benefit greatly from federal programs—44 percent of Louisiana's state budget comes from the federal government, yet they voted for Tea Party candidates who support tax breaks for big business, massive reductions in state spending for education, healthcare, and environmental quality with most of the benefits going to out-of-state and international firms and few profits staying in their state.

Arlie Hochschild found an answer to the Great Paradox. Economically, culturally, and politically, Tea Party members and millions of other Americans like them suddenly found themselves strangers in their own land, and Trump provided a path to redemption—an opportunity to feel pride instead of shame. Together they shared a collective effervescence—a state of emotional excitement felt by those who join with others to be members of a moral or biological tribe. Simply, they voted, not for their economic best interest, but for their emotional and cultural self interest.

Final Thoughts

Americans are now more divided than we have been since the eve of the Civil War. We are in the midst of a cold civil war. We are two societies, separate but unequal, caught in a reinforcing cycle of division that is difficult to break. The divisions are deep—social, economic, cultural, and geographical—but they are essential to understanding the nation's political realignment. Understanding these changes is necessary to understand better our nation's immigration policy. Immigration is a process that shapes our national character—what it means to be an American. These changes are why the debate is so intense and why political solutions seem to be impossible. Tragically, more than one million young people are caught in the middle. Brought here as children, they were educated in our schools, socialized in our neighborhoods, and now, as adults, are contributing their education and skills to growing our economy. In the months to come, they will be in peril of deportation, they will lose their jobs, and they will move back into the shadows of our society. With this as our backdrop, the rest of the book explores our immigration history; the policy known as Deferred Action for Childhood Arrivals (DACA); the effectiveness of the program; the hopes, dreams, and challenges of the young people to whom we have awarded DACA protections; profiles of two Dreamers; and next steps—how we pass a law that protects them.

TWO

If Truth Be Told

Facts on Today's Immigration

During the 2016 presidential race, the candidates from both parties quickly staked out their positions on immigration, and the subject emerged as a dominant domestic-policy issue during the election. Hillary Clinton and Donald Trump's views were on the opposite ends of the spectrum. Clinton supported a pathway to citizenship for the millions of undocumented residents in the United States and promised that she would shield millions more from deportation through Deferred Action for Parents of Americans (DAPA). Trump, in contrast, stated that amnesty was unfair to people who had been waiting in line for years and that anyone in this country illegally—regardless of age—would be deported. On all the major immigration issues—deportation, guest workers, H1-B visas, border security, or sanctuary cities—the two candidates gave the American electorate a stark choice on the immigration issue.[1]

What I find interesting is that immigration and immigration policy are incredibly complicated issues that have profound consequences for our society, yet in the 2016 election the candidates focused on just one facet of the issue—illegal immigration. And when the candidates strayed from their core message, they often muddled the facts. The Pulitzer Prize-winning website PolitiFact.com found misstatements on both sides. This section attempts to clarify the facts about immigration by using government data and reports from nonpartisan research organizations such as the Migration Policy Institute and the Pew Research Center. In a question and answer format, we will explore the facts of our nation's immigration history.

Facts About US Immigration History You May Not Know

Has the United States always had immigration controls?

No. Although the federal government has the sole responsibility for determining who enters our nation, for much of our history our immigration policy was laissez-faire. This changed in 1891 with the creation of the Office of Superintendent of Immigration in the Treasury Department. The new service opened Ellis Island in New York on January 2, 1892. Passports weren't required until 1918, and were used only for identification at that time.[2]

What about illegal immigration?

The concept of "illegality" didn't exist until the creation of the US Border Patrol in 1924 when entry without inspection was prohibited, and a deportation policy became permanent. The Emergency Quota Act of 1921 and the Immigration Act of 1924, together known as "The Quota Acts," restricted immigration from most countries outside of Northern and Western Europe.[3]

Friends have used companies like Ancestry DNA and Family Tree DNA and point with pride to their roots in Great Britain and Western Europe. They tell me their ancestors came here "the right way!" If their ancestors came before 1924, their assumptions are wrong. The US government didn't require visas for entry until the passage of the Immigration Act of 1924.[4]

Donald Trump wants to "build a wall" across our southern border. Has immigration from Mexico always been a problem?

The first Mexican "immigrants" didn't cross a border, rather the border crossed them; they were living here before we annexed the Southwest. Until 1924, the border between the United States and Mexico was largely unpoliced, migration flowed openly, and transnational families were common.

The Current Wave of Immigration

How many foreign-born people live in the United States?

There are approximately 43.7 million foreign-born people living in the United States. When you add the forty million children who have at least one foreign-born parent, 25 percent of the US population is a first- or second-generation immigrant. The United States has the largest immigrant population in the world with 19.8 percent of the world's total foreign-born population. Germany and Russia are second and third with around twelve million immigrants or 5 percent of their populations.[5]

How has our foreign-born population changed over the past half century?

The Immigration Act of 1965 ended the quota system and marked the beginning of the nation's Fourth Wave of Immigration. Since then,

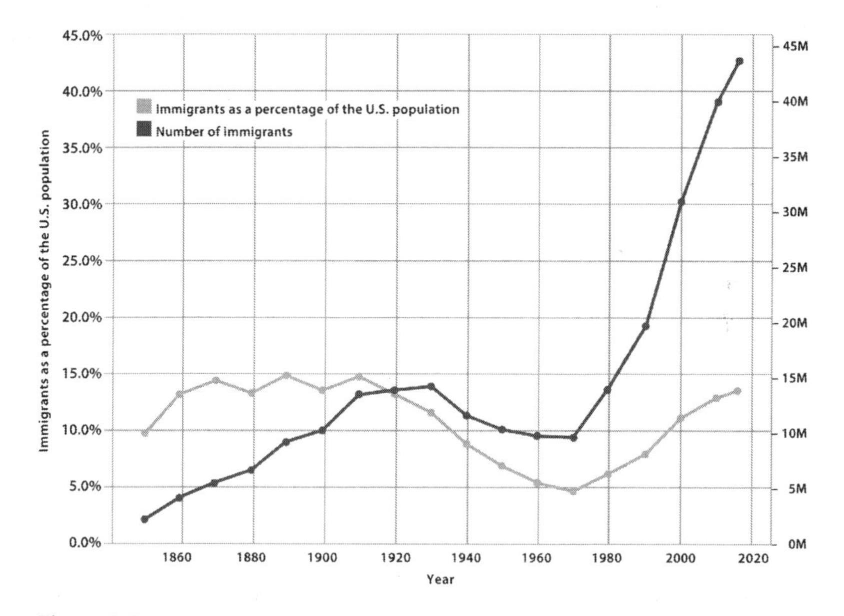

Figure 2.1

US Immigration Population and Share Over Time, 1850–Present Staff.

Source: Staff. (2016). "US Immigration Trends," Migration Policy Institute, https://www.migrationpolicy.org/programs/data-hub/us-immigration-trends, accessed November 15, 2017.

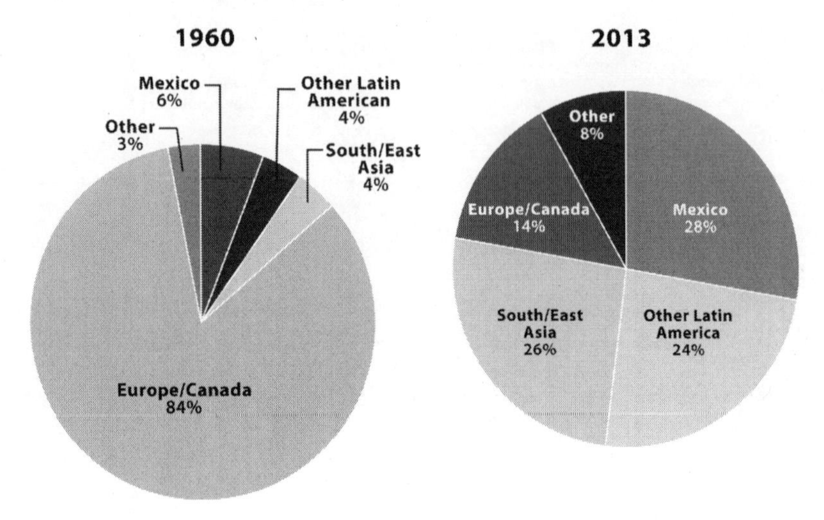

Figure 2.2

US Immigrant Population by World Region of Birth, 1960–2015.

Source: Staff. "US Immigration Trends." Migration Policy Institute," https://www.migrationpolicy.org/programs/data-hub/us-immigration-trends, accessed November 15, 2018.

our foreign-born population has quadrupled. Today, 13.5 percent of our population is foreign-born, but it is still below the late nineteenth-century peak of 14.8 percent.[6]

Has the source of our immigration changed?

Yes. Significantly. In 1970, 75 percent of the foreign-born population living in the United States was from Europe; today most of our immigrants come from Latin America and Asia. In 2015, 11.6 million foreign-born residents (26.9 percent of the foreign-born population) were from Mexico; 2.7 million immigrants were from China; 2.4 million were from India; 2 million were from the Philippines; 1.4 million were from El Salvador; 1.3 million were from Vietnam; 1.2 million were from Cuba; and 1.1 million each from the Dominican Republic and South Korea.[7]

How have immigrants changed the nation's racial and ethnic makeup?

In 1965, our population was 84 percent white, 11 percent black, 4 percent Hispanic, and 1 percent Asian. Today, the black share of our population is the same, but the Hispanic population has grown to 18 percent and Asian population to 6 percent, while the white share has fallen to 62 percent. By midcentury, the United States is projected to have no racial or ethnic majority.[7]

Where do most immigrants live?

Most immigrants with legal permanent residency in the Fourth Wave live in cities in the traditional gateway states of California (20 percent), New York (12.4 percent), Florida (11.3 percent), Texas (9.5 percent), and New Jersey (4.7 percent). However, beginning in the 1990s, new arrivals began to settle in less-traditional immigrant states like North Carolina, Alabama, Arkansas, Kansas, and Nebraska.[8]

How are immigrants doing? Are they weaving into the fabric of American society?

Yes, and the evidence suggests that immigrants are moving into the mainstream faster than Third Wave Immigrants from Southern and Eastern Europe and Asia who arrived here a century ago.

How do we know that immigrants are integrating into American society?

Social scientists use four variables to measure integration: residential segregation, upward mobility, speaking English, and intermarriage. Studies show that our newest immigrants integrate like previous immigrants, but at a faster rate.[10]

Are immigrants segregated in their own neighborhoods and ethnic enclaves?

The 2010 census revealed that Asian and Latino immigrants have moderate degrees of segregation, much lower than the segregation of blacks. Although these patterns haven't changed much in the past three decades, the data support integration. When the data are grouped by generation, second-generation Asians and Hispanics are less segregated than first generation, and subsequent generations have even lower levels of segregation.[11]

Are immigrants becoming a permanent underclass?

No. Most research shows that the socioeconomic status of the second- and third-generation immigrants, regardless of their race and ethnicity, do better than the first generation. Here are a few facts:[12]

- Fewer than one-in-five immigrants live in poverty as compared to the general population.
- Immigrant men have higher employment rates than US-born men, and their wages rise the longer they live in the United States.
- Immigrant children have higher wages than their parents, experience greater upward mobility, and are less likely to live in poverty than their parents.
- Compared with all Americans, US-born children of immigrants are more likely to go to college, less likely to live in poverty, and equally likely to be homeowners.

Are immigrants learning English?

Immigrants learn English faster than the immigrants who came to the United States at the turn of the last century. Fewer than half of all immigrants who arrived in the United States between 1900 and 1920 spoke English within their first five years after immigrating while more than three-quarters who arrived between 1980 and 2000 spoke English within the first five years.[13]

Do immigrants tend to marry people of the same background?

Marriage is the most intimate relationship that we enter into during our lives. Intermarriage is the bellwether of integration. Yes, immigrants tend to marry someone of the same ethnic group, but approximately 26 percent of Hispanics and 28 percent of Asians married outside their ethnic group between 2008 and 2010. This is higher than couples in the Third Wave. Intermarriage rates between groups suggest that social barriers between ethnic groups are quite thin.

So, what do we make of these trends?

Integration is occurring. Whether it be where the current immigrants live, the education they receive, the jobs they acquire, the incomes they earn, the language they speak, or the people they marry, the current wave of immigrants is integrating faster than the earlier waves of immigrants. And you see this process among the nation's Hispanic population in figure 2.3. By the fourth generation, half of our population with

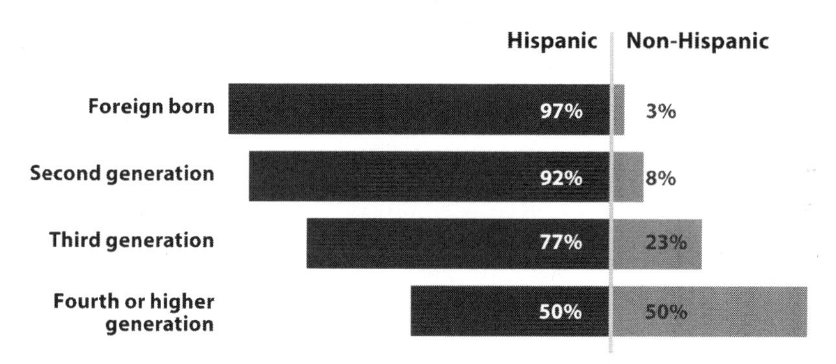

Figure 2.3

Hispanic Identity Declines over Generations.

Source: Washington, S. 2017. "Among Americans with Hispanic Ancestry, Share that Identifies as Hispanic or Latino Falls across Immigrant Generations." Pew Research Center, http://www.pewhispanic.org/2017/12/20/hispanic-identity-fades-across-generations-as-immigrant-connections-fall-away/ph_2017-12-20_hispanic-identity_01/, accessed November 15, 2017.

Hispanic ancestry no longer identifies as Hispanic or Latino—they see themselves as Americans.

Impact of Immigrants on the US Economy

Throughout the political campaign, some candidates told us that immigrants are a drain on our economy. Is that true?

Far from it. The Selig Center for Economic Growth reports that the nation's total buying power reached $13.9 trillion in 2016. Hispanic buying power was $1.4 trillion and accounted for nearly 10 percent of the US total. Framed another way, the US Hispanic market is larger than the Gross Domestic Product (GDP) of Mexico and all but fourteen other countries in the world. The data for Asian Americans is even more impressive. Making up only 6 percent of our population, they accounted for $1.4 trillion of the nation's buying power in 2016. Their buying power exceeds the economies of all but fifteen countries in the world.[14] Another startling statistic—40 percent of Fortune 500 companies were founded by a first or second-generation immigrant (figure 2.4).[15]

So, immigrants make a contribution to our economy, but are they taking our jobs?

No. Research has consistently shown that immigrants complement, rather than compete, with US-born workers. American and immigrant workers have different skill sets and tend to work in different jobs and industries, even when they have similar educational backgrounds.[16] Research on the impact of immigrant labor on wages has similar findings. Immigrants consume goods and services, creating jobs for natives and other immigrants alike thus increasing the average wages of US-born workers by 0.4 percent.[17]

There is another important part of this story—our rapidly aging labor force. On January 1, 2011, the oldest members of the Baby Boomer generation turned sixty-five, and an additional ten thousand boomers will reach retirement age each day for the next twenty years.

Industry	Number of companies	Percent of industry total
High Tech	45	46%
Wholesale / Retail	37	43%
Finance / Insurance	26	33%
Industrials	23	56%
Consumer Goods	20	49%
Energy	19	32%
Transportation	18	51%
Bsuiness Services	14	64%
Media / Entertainment	9	56%
Healthcare	5	24%

Figure 2.4

Immigrant- and Immigrant-Offspring-Founded Fortune 500 Companies by Industry.

Source: Florida, R. 2017. "Without Immigrants, the Fortune 500 Would Be the Fortune 284." CityLab, https://www.citylab.com/equity/2017/12/without-immigrants-the-fortune-500-would-be-the-fortune-284/547421/, accessed February 12, 2018.

A quarter of our population are members of this cohort, and their retirements and deaths will dramatically change the composition of our population.[18] In the next decade, seven million US-born workers are expected to leave the labor force, and immigrants and their children will fill the gap. Looking to the future, from 2015 to 2065, immigrants and their descendants are expected to account for 88 percent of US population growth.[19] As such, immigrants and their children will be critical in replacing retiring workers, giving the United States the youngest workforce in the developing world and a competitive advantage over rapidly aging countries like China, Russia, and those in the European Union.

In Millions

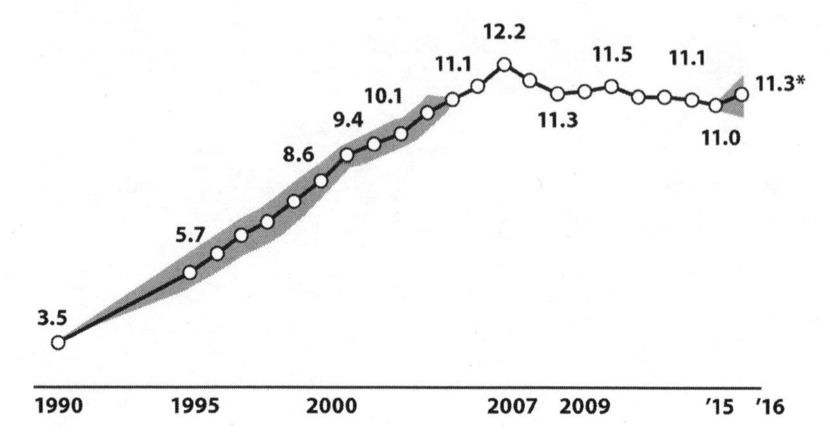

Figure 2.5

US Unauthorized Immigrant Population, 1990–2016.

Source: Passel, J. S., and D. Cohn, 2017. "As Mexican Share Declined, US Unauthorized Immigrant Population Fell in 2015 Below Recession Level." Pew Research Center, http:/www.pewresearch.org/fact-tank/2017/04/25/as-mexican-share-declined-u-s-unauthorized-immigrant-population-fell-in-2015-below-recession-level/, accessed November 15, 2017.

Unauthorized Immigrants

How many unauthorized immigrants are in the United States?

The unauthorized population has declined slightly in recent years after rapid growth for decades. In 2016, there were an estimated 11.3 million unauthorized immigrants residing in the United States. This population reached a high of 12.2 million in 2007, but saw a gradual decline during the Great Recession.[20]

How serious is unauthorized immigration across our southern border?

Mexicans account for half of all unauthorized immigrants in the United States, but the unauthorized Mexican population is declining. In 2014, 5.8 million unauthorized immigrants from Mexico resided in the United States, compared with 6.4 million in 2009 and 6.9 million in

2007.[21] More Mexicans are returning home than arriving in the United States, due, in large part, to an improving Mexican economy and recently implemented social reforms. In the past decade, one million immigrants returned to Mexico while 870,000 arrived in the United States. Much of this drop is attributable to a drop in unauthorized Mexican immigrants, and most unauthorized arrivals today are from other parts of Latin America. Enhanced border security and Trump's harsh immigration rhetoric have also contributed to this decline.[22]

With the billions spent on border control, why are unauthorized immigrants still crossing our border?

Their strategy has changed. Increasingly unauthorized immigrants are entering the United States legally and overstaying visas rather than crossing the border. In 2014, 42 percent of the unauthorized population—around 4.5 million individuals—held expired visas. Visa overstays have exceeded unauthorized border crossings every year from 2007 through 2014 and, over this period, a total of six hundred thousand more individuals overstayed visas than entered the United States by illegally crossing the border.[23]

Do we really need the border wall?

The data don't support it. Apprehensions at the US-Mexico border are at a historic low. Border agents now patrol every mile of the southern border daily, and in many places they can view nearly all attempts to cross the border in real time. In 2016, there were 408,870 border apprehensions, an increase from the 331,333 that took place in 2015. In 2017, after an initial increase from October through January, apprehensions decreased substantially in February and March, and hit a historic low in April 2017.[24] Current apprehension levels remain among the lowest experienced since the 1970s.[25]

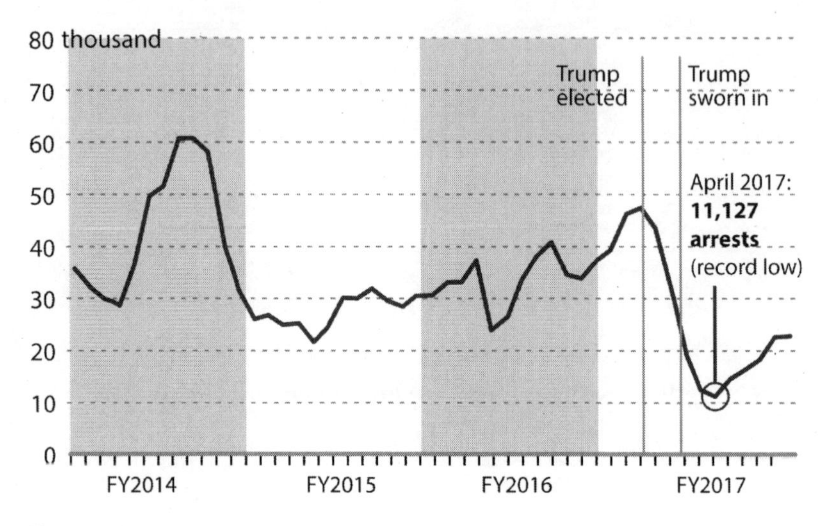

Figure 2.6

Southwest Border Arrests by Month since 2014.

Source: Department of Homeland Security. 2017. "Southwest Border Total Apprehensions/Inadmissibles, FY12–17." US Customs and Border Protection, https://www.cbp.gov/sites/default/files/assets/documents/2017-Dec/CBP%20 Apprehensions.pdf, accessed January 10, 2017.

What are the destinations of the unauthorized immigrants?

Most have settled in the cities in traditional gateway states of California (21 percent); Texas (15 percent); Florida (8 percent); New York (7 percent); New Jersey (5 percent); and Illinois (4 percent).[26]

Where are unauthorized immigrants from?

Mexico and Central America account for 7.9 million or 71 percent of the unauthorized immigrants in the United States. About 1.5 million (13 percent) were from Asia; 673,000 (6 percent) from South America; 432,000 (4 percent) from Europe, Canada, or Oceania; 353,000 (3 percent) from Africa; and 232,000 (2 percent) from the Caribbean.[27]

How long have they lived here?

The majority of unauthorized immigrants are long-term residents of the United States with 66 percent of them having lived in the United States for ten years or longer.[28]

Do they join other family members once they arrive here?

Unauthorized immigrants are often part of the same family as authorized immigrants and native-born Americans. There are seven million people living in mixed-status families—those with at least one unauthorized immigrant—including 9.6 million adults and 5.9 million children who are US citizens.[29] Deporting an unauthorized immigrant means disrupting the lives of whole families and the communities in which they live.

Are unauthorized immigrants eligible for Social Security and Medicare?

No. But they pay into the trust funds for which they receive few benefits. In 2010, unauthorized immigrants paid $13 billion into Social Security and received only $1 billion in services—a net contribution of $12 billion.[30] From 2000 to 2011, unauthorized immigrants contributed $2.2 to $3.8 billion more than they withdrew annually from Medicare's Trust Fund (a total surplus of $35.1 billion).[31]

Do unauthorized immigrants pay state and local taxes?

Yes. They pay more than $7 billion in sales and excise taxes, $3.6 billion in property taxes, and nearly $1.1 billion in personal income taxes. Granting all unauthorized immigrants legal status would boost their tax contributions an additional $2.2 billion per year. Immigrants—even legal immigrants—pay to support many of the benefits they are barred from receiving.[32]

What would be the cost of the mass deportation of all unauthorized immigrants?

It is estimated that the removal of unauthorized immigrants from the workforce would lead to a 2.6 percent decline in GDP—an average annual loss of $434 billion. This policy would reduce the GDP $4.7 trillion over ten years, and mass deportation would cost the federal government nearly $900 billion in lost revenue over ten years. Additionally, there would be severe labor shortages in several economic sectors.[33] Houston, following Hurricane Harvey, is a good example. Most of the city's contractors could not find the labor needed to rebuild homes, offices, and businesses because undocumented workers, fearing deportation, were afraid to work in the city. This is in sharp contrast with the rebuilding of New Orleans after Katrina where immigrants, authorized and unauthorized, provided much of the labor.

Deferred Action for Childhood Arrival

What is Deferred Action for Childhood Arrivals or DACA?

The program, known as DACA, was created through an executive action by President Obama on June 15, 2012.[34] It gives unauthorized immigrants who were brought to the United States before age sixteen a chance to stay here to study or work, provided they meet certain conditions such as being enrolled in high school or having a high school degree or GED equivalent and not having a serious criminal or multiple misdemeanor convictions. Those approved for the program have been given a work permit and protection from deportation for two years. The benefits could be renewed.[35]

How many unauthorized youth have benefited from the program?

The Migration Policy Institute estimates that in 2016, 1.3 million young adults ages fifteen and older were immediately eligible to apply for DACA. The number rose to 1.7 million when the additional 398,000 unauthorized youth who had met all the criteria except high school graduation or current school enrollment were added.[36] However, the Pew

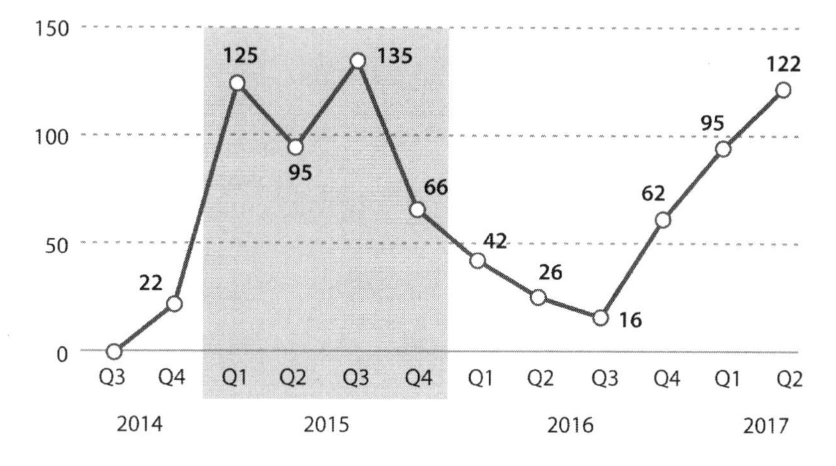

Note: Totals are applications approved for renewal of Deferrred Action for Childhood Arrivals program benefits, which can be renewed every two years.

Figure 2.7

Dreamers Awarded Extended Deportation Relief and Work Permits Number of DACA Renewal Applications Accepted, in Thousands.

Source: Krogstad, J. M. 2017. "DACA Has Shielded Nearly 790,000 Young Unauthorized Immigrants from Deportation." Pew Research Center, http://www.pewresearch.org/fact-tank/2017/09/01/unauthorized-immigrants-covered-by-daca-face-uncertain-future/, accessed January 26, 2018.

Research Center reported that only 690,000 unauthorized immigrants were enrolled in DACA as of September 4, 2017. Roughly 800,000 unauthorized immigrants have received DACA, but almost 110,000 of this group are no longer enrolled in the program.[37]

Why have so many DACA recipients been dropped from the program?

About seventy thousand former DACA participants did not renew their benefits or had their renewal applications denied. Many of those not reapplying thought the program was ending, and others feared their personal information would be used to track them and other family members for deportation. Another forty thousand obtained green cards that granted them lawful permanent residence.[38]

Is DACA being phased out?

Yes. The program is being phased out. The Trump administration rescinded President Obama's executive order on September 5, 2017.[39] A federal district court has stayed the order, but DACA will probably end when the case is heard in the US Supreme Court.

What will happen to these young people?

The rescission of the DACA program was to go into effect beginning on March 6, 2018. Recent federal district court rulings have stayed its rescission which means these young people live in limbo waiting rulings by the appellate courts. If the appellate courts side with the Trump administration, unauthorized youth will begin losing their work authorization and protection from deportation through March 5, 2020.[40]

What will be the impact?

The average DACA recipient arrived in the United States when they were six years old and are now in their midtwenties. Many are married with children and have jobs, homes, and cars—they are living the American Dream. They are part of neighborhoods and communities with networks of families and friends. They earn more, buy more, and pay more taxes. This comes to an end when their DACA expires because they will be unemployed and face deportation. The cost to our nation is a loss of the human capital educated and trained in the United States. And the Cato Institute, a libertarian think tank, estimates the cost of deporting people currently in the DACA program would be more than $60 billion to the federal government along with a $280 billion reduction in economic growth over the next decade.[41]

What has DACA done for the nation's economy?

DACA increased recipients' average hourly wages by 42 percent, and allowed many to move into jobs with better pay and working conditions. A further 6 percent started their own business. With better jobs and higher wages, many individuals purchased cars and homes, leading to more state and local revenue in the form of property and sales taxes.[42]

What are the costs of ending DACA recipients' work permits and forcing them out of the labor force?

As of November 2016, 645,000 DACA recipients are employed. It is estimated that the cost would be $433.4 billion in GDP and would decrease Social Security and Medicare contributions by $24.6 billion over the next decade.[43]

How would the United States benefit economically if immigration reform that includes a path to citizenship is passed?

Such reform would increase the GDP $1.2 trillion over 10 years and create 145,000 jobs annually. Americans' income would increase by a cumulative $625 billion.[44]

What Americans Think about Immigration

Immigration has long been a contentious issue in our society. In the late nineteenth and early twentieth century, the nation's angst was over the millions of Eastern and Southern Europeans and Asians arriving on our shores. Different in culture, appearance, and religion from the native population with Northern and Western European roots, the federal government passed race-based immigration laws to keep them out. Much is the same today with the Fourth Wave, and once again the federal government is passing laws and enacting policies designed to reduce immigration from Latin America, the Middle East, Africa, and Asia. But are our elected officials passing laws and creating policies that reflect the will of the American people? The Gallup Organization conducted a series of polls on immigration in 2017 that answers these questions.

What do Americans think about our current level of immigration?

As a whole, Americans' attitudes about immigration haven't changed significantly since Donald Trump became president. Americans remain about as likely to say they would like to see immigration kept at its present level (38 percent), as they are to say it should be decreased (35 percent). About one in four say immigration should be increased (24 percent).[45]

Do Americans think immigrants are taking American jobs?

In general, US adults say immigrants take jobs Americans don't want. Public concern about immigrants' effects on the economy may be even less pronounced than it appears to be. Gallup asks respondents if they think immigrants take jobs that Americans want or if they take low-paying jobs that US adults aren't interested in. By a commanding margin, 72 percent said immigrants take jobs Americans don't want over the 18 percent who say immigrants take jobs US adults want.[46]

Do Americans think immigration is affecting their jobs and companies?

According to studies, it's most Americans' view that immigrants have a positive impact on the economy and that they take jobs others don't want. Most adults don't see immigrants having a negative effect on their own careers. A Gallup poll found that 60 percent of respondents say immigration has no effect on their own job, and 54 percent believe it isn't affecting the business or organization they work for.[47]

What about immigration's impact on our economy?

Given the Trump administration's tough policy on immigrants, it is not surprising that members of his party are less likely to say immigrants help the economy. Democrats are more likely to say immigrants help the economy (59 percent) than Republicans (28 percent). This is in contrast to the last time Gallup asked this question. In 2005, when 40 percent of Democrats said immigration would mostly help the economy, while 35 percent of Republicans said the same.[48]

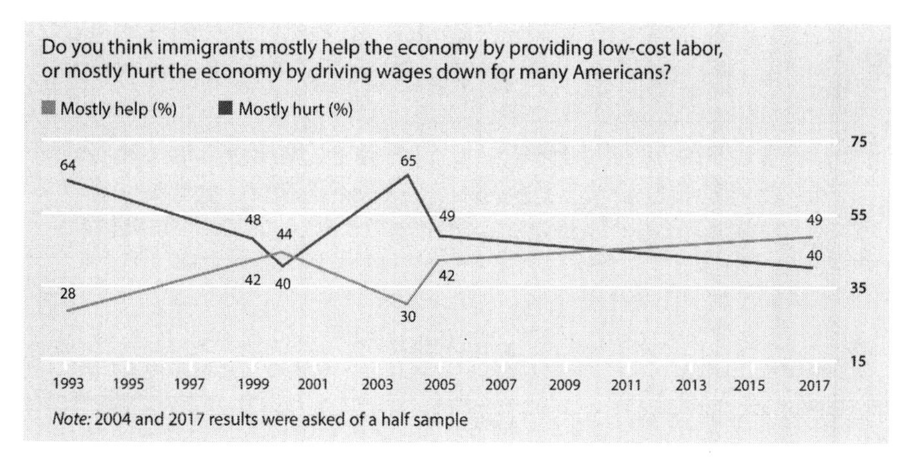

Figure 2.8

Americans Say Immigrants Mostly Help the US

Final Thoughts

As this chapter has shown, we are a nation of immigrants, and today there are 43.7 million immigrants living in our midst. When you add the forty million people with at least one foreign-born parent, one-out-of-four people living in the nation is a first- or second- generation immigrant. We have not seen these numbers in a century.

Four waves of immigration have shaped our national character. The immigrants from Western and Northern Europe dominated the first two waves, but the source of immigration shifted to Southern and Eastern Europe and Asia in the late nineteenth century, then to the Americas and Asia beginning late in the twentieth. These cultural and racial differences are at the heart of our current debate on immigration. However, there is overwhelming evidence that the immigrants in the newest wave are being integrated into the fabric of our society faster than earlier groups.

Although many Americans oppose our current immigration levels, it is a process essential to our nation's renewal. Whether we look at the buying power of authorized and unauthorized immigrants, their labor force participation, the taxes they pay, or the contributions they make to the Social Security and Medicare Trust funds, they are a potent force in our economy. Deporting the unauthorized would shrink our labor force, and the nation's GDP would decline 2.6 percent. Although immigration is a complicated issue, our political discourse has focused on a minor part—unauthorized immigration—and youth brought to this country by their parents as children have become pawns in this debate.

This chapter is the backdrop for the discussion to comc on immigration policy and DACA. As we will see, DACA has been successful. By removing the threat of deportation and providing work authorization, these young people have come out of the shadows and fully participated in our society. And, there is urgency in finding a political solution; the Trump administration has ended the program. Although a federal judge has reinstated the program for now, DACAmented youth will continue to live in peril of losing their deferments until there is a legislative solution. The next chapter explores how the DACA policy came to be and how it ended.

THREE

The Nation's Immigration Law

The DREAM Act and DACA

> [In] the best interests of our country, and in keeping with the obligations of my office, the Department of Homeland Security will begin an orderly transition and wind-down of DACA, one that provides minimum disruption. . . . This is a gradual process, not a sudden phase out. . . . Thus, in effect, I am not going to just cut DACA off, but rather provide a window of opportunity for Congress to finally act. . . . As I've said before, we will resolve the DACA issue with heart and compassion—but through the lawful democratic process—while at the same time ensuring that any immigration reform we adopt provides enduring benefits for the American citizens we were elected to serve.[1]

This statement released by the Trump administration on September 5, 2017, struck fear in the hearts of eight hundred thousand DACAmented youth. The average DACA recipient was brought here at the age of six and is now in her/his midtwenties. Sixty-five percent of them are in high school or college, and 90 percent of them work. Many are married, some with children who are US citizens, and all face the specter of unemployment and deportation beginning on March 5, 2018, as their deferments expire.[2]

Congress's first attempt to solve the problem of undocumented youth was the **D**evelopment, **R**elief, and **E**ducation for **A**lien **M**inors Act, the DREAM Act, introduced by US Senators Dick Durbin (D-Illinois) and Orrin Hatch (R-Utah) on August 1, 2001 (S. 1291). The bill, if it had become law, would have first granted qualifying undocumented minors conditional residency and, upon meeting further qualifications, permanent residency and a path to citizenship. Although the DREAM Act had the overwhelming support of the American people across political parties, it failed to pass in the 107th Congress and subsequent ones.[3]

How did our society reach this point? How have we allowed young people who reside in our communities, attend our schools, play on our teams, worship in our churches, speak our language, work in our businesses, and think of themselves as Americans to live in limbo? In this chapter, we explore how our policies on undocumented youth have evolved.

A Short History of Immigration Law

If the US Congress and the president could formulate a coherent immigration policy, it would look something like this: We would have secure borders; highly skilled foreign nationals could be hired quickly and gain permanent residency and their immediate family could join them in a few years; international students in strategic fields could choose to stay in this country when they graduate and employers could hire foreign workers to fill the unskilled jobs Americans will not do; foreign entrepreneurs could easily start businesses here; unauthorized adults could earn residency status; and undocumented youth, brought here as children, could gain permanent residency and a path to citizenship. If this policy existed, there would be no need for this book. The truth is that we have a contradictory, incoherent, and unfair set of policies that do not reflect the nation's economic and social needs or our values.

The Chinese Exclusion Act of 1882 is a good starting point for understanding our current impasse on immigration reform. It was racist—the nation's first law to prevent a specific ethnic group from immigrating to the United States. The rationale for its passage was that Chinese people endangered the good order of certain localities.[4] The reality was that Congress was responding to West Coast politicians pressured by the racial concerns of their constituents. It was partisan and parochial, and these same forces frame our current immigration debate.[5]

Following in the steps of the Chinese Exclusion Act, Congress established a new immigration policy and a national-origins quota system with the enactment of the Quota Laws in 1921 and 1924. These laws restricted immigration by nationality to a quota based on the group's representation in the US Census. The outcome was that people from Northern European countries had a higher quota and were more likely to be admitted to the United States than people from Eastern and Southern Europe or other non-European countries. Forty years later, Congress passed the Immigration and Nationality Act of 1965, which abolished the national-origins quota system and established preferences for relatives of US citizens and lawful permanent residents and for immigrants with specific job skills. These policies are still largely in place, and the passage of the 1965 act marks the beginning of this nation's Fourth Wave of Immigration.[6]

Immigration levels swelled after the passage of the 1965 act. During the 1940s only 856,608 immigrants entered the country; but by the end of the 1960s, this number had swelled to 3.2 million. In subsequent decades, the number grew to 4.2 million in the 1970s, 6.2 million in the 1980s, 9.8 million in the 1990s, 10.3 million in the 2000s, and the numbers will be even higher by the end of this decade.[7]

There has been a parallel growth of unauthorized immigrants. In 1970, the US Census estimated that there were five hundred thousand unauthorized immigrants in the country—just .3 percent of the immigrant population. The unauthorized population rose rapidly during the 1990s and 2000s, from an estimated 3.5 million in 1990s, to a peak of 12.2 million in 2007, to an estimated 11.1 million unauthorized immigrants in 2016. This population has remained stable for the past few years after nearly two decades of constant change.[8]

Congress responded to the growing number of unauthorized immigrants with the passage of the Immigration Reform and Control Act of 1986. The law sought to enhance enforcement and to create new pathways to legal immigration. Congress imposed sanctions on employers who knowingly hired or recruited unauthorized aliens. More important, the law created amnesty programs for the unauthorized, and roughly 2.7 million people residing illegally in the United States became lawful permanent residents.[9] There was another significant development during this decade—the Supreme Court's 1982 *Plyler v. Doe* ruling that deemed undocumented children blameless for the violation of immigration law by their parents. As a result, there was now a legal distinction between undocumented children and their parents. The court based its decision on the premise that education is necessary for full participation in our society, and it was in our national interest that all children, regardless of immigration status, be provided public education. The *Plyler* decision shaped the DREAM Act.[10]

Even with these developments, the numbers of undocumented continued to swell, and in response to continuing concerns about unauthorized immigration, Congress passed two major immigration laws in the 1990s—The Personal Responsibility and Work Opportunity Reconciliation Act of 1996 (PRWORA) and the Illegal Immigration Reform and Immigrant Responsibility Act (IIRIRA). These laws addressed several immigration concerns of that time: removing incentives for illegal immigration, limiting benefits for those here illegally, and barring illegal immigrants' employment in high-skilled jobs. Congress also codified the distinction between children and their parents, with the result that once children reach eighteen, the law requires them to correct their undocumented status. They can't. The unintended consequence was that millions of undocumented youth face deportation when they reached eighteen, and their plight led to the DREAM Act and DACA.[11]

Our democracy addresses the practical concerns of our people. Congress should write legislation that reflects our wishes mindful of the economic, social, and political forces at work in our society. But the nature of our democracy is that it is slow to respond to problems, politicians tend to take the path of least resistance, and in our current hyperpartisan climate, the immigration laws tend to mirror the concerns of special interests and not the people affected by them. The outcome is a flawed and self-serving legislation. An excellent example of our current dysfunctional legislative process is the DREAM Act and President Obama's solution to the political impasse with his executive order, Deferred Action for Childhood Arrivals (DACA).

The Development Relief and Education for Alien Minors (DREAM) Act

In a much-anticipated announcement, on September 5, 2017, Attorney General Jeff Sessions announced the recission of DACA, a signature Obama administration executive action that made nearly two million unauthorized immigrant youth potentially eligible for temporary relief from deportation along with lawful employment. The Trump administration's attorney general called it an "unconstitutional exercise of authority." With 680,000 DACA recipients set to begin losing their protection in March 2018, a firestorm of protests followed the announcement from across the country—immigration activists, members of Congress from both sides of the aisle, governors, leaders in the technology industry, CEOs of Fortune 500 companies, university presidents, and religious leaders. Additionally, polls indicate broad public support for immigration reform that includes a path to citizenship.[12]

In his September 5 announcement, President Trump stated, "I am not going to just cut DACA off, but rather provide a window of opportunity for Congress to finally act. . . . As I've said before, we will resolve the DACA issue with heart and compassion." The pundits have speculated that the six-month deadline in the administration's announcement was designed to force Congress to come up with a long-term legislative fix, something that has eluded it for the past seventeen years. They may be right but don't hold your breath. As of October 2017, members of Congress from both political parties have filed five reform bills.[13] So what are the DREAM Act and DACA? How are they related? Let's take a more detailed look.

The Development Relief and Education for Alien Minors (DREAM) Act is designed to allow undocumented immigrant youth who were brought to the United States as children to obtain conditional lawful permanent resident (LPR) status if they remain in high school, receive a degree (or GED), and go on to college or join the military. The 2017 version of the DREAM Act would permit students to obtain conditional LPR status if they satisfy the following conditions.

- Are undocumented, a DACA recipient, or a Temporary Protective Status (TPS) beneficiary,
- Entered the United States before the age of eighteen,
- Been continuously present in the country for at least four years prior to the bill's enactment,
- Obtained a high school degree or a GED or admitted to an institution of higher learning,
- Have no convictions for certain criminal offenses,
- Pass a medical exam, and
- Pass a background check.

Undocumented students who satisfy these conditions would be able to apply for up to eight years of conditional legal permanent status, which would allow them to work, travel, attend college, or join the military. If, within this eight-year period, she or he completes at least two years toward a four-year degree, graduates from a two-year college, or serves at least two years in the military, and maintains good moral character, the conditional status would be removed and the person would be granted permanent resident status and be eligible for US citizenship. In the bill's latest version, DREAM Act students would not be eligible for public benefits but college affordability is improved by changes in the rules that limit their access to in-state tuition and the student financial aid made available by states and institutions.

Senators Orrin Hatch, R-UT, and Richard Durbin, D-IL, introduced the DREAM Act in 2001. It failed to pass the Senate. Since then multiple DREAM Act bills have been introduced to address the plight of undocumented students. In July 2003, Senators Hatch and Durbin reintroduced the legislation with strong bipartisan support (there were forty-eight co-sponsors from both parties), but the bill never made it to the Senate floor. In the House, 152 members on both sides of the aisle sponsored a similar bill. It too failed. In the 111th Congress, the House approved DREAM Act language in an unrelated bill, but it failed in the Senate on a 55 to 41 vote, five votes short of invoking cloture. In the 112th Congress, legislation was introduced in both houses with bipartisan co-sponsorship (H 1842 and S 952), and hearings were held but there was no action by either house. The most recent attempt began on July 20, 2017, when Senator Lindsey Graham (R-SC) introduced the DREAM Act of 2017 (S.1615) with co-sponsors from both parties.

Support for the DREAM Act remains high among the general public. In a March 7, 2017, Gallup Poll, when asked if illegal immigrants should be given the chance to become US citizens, more than 75 percent of Republicans and 90 percent of Democrats agreed that they should. And tracking polls like the NBC News / Wall Street Journal Poll, as well as surveys by nonpartisan groups like the Migration Policy Institute and the Pew Research Center, show consistent support for a path to citizenship for undocumented youth. In addition, many of the nation's labor, political, and business organizations have long supported the legislation. Simply, the Congress is out of touch with the

American people as attested to by historically low approval ratings.[14] And with Congress in gridlock, President Obama addressed immigration and the cause of undocumented youth through his use of executive orders.

Congress passes laws and the executive branch executes them. Executive orders have been used since the presidency of George Washington to manage the operations of the federal government, and have the force of law.[15] Before he became president, Donald Trump accused former President Obama of abusing his power by signing so many executive orders. But according to the American Presidency Project, Trump signed thirty executive orders in his first one hundred days, eleven more than signed by former President Obama during the same time frame and nineteen more than former President George W. Bush. Trump signed forty-two executive orders in his first two hundred days, significantly more than former presidents Obama (twenty-two), G. W. Bush (twenty-four), and Clinton (twenty-five) in the same time period.[16] Most of Trump's executive orders reversed Obama administration policies, including the one that created DACA.

The Obama Administration Responds to Congressional Gridlock

Few Americans are aware that the Obama administration addressed our broken immigration system through executive action, a presidential power based on the principle of administrative discretion. Presidents, governors, judges, and administrative heads have limited resources to address problems, so they are permitted by law to make discretionary decisions in the discharge of their public duties as long as their decisions can be reviewed by another branch of government. In 2014, the president asked then secretary of homeland security Jeh Johnson and then attorney general Eric Holder to undertake a rigorous and inclusive review to inform recommendations on reforming our broken immigration system through executive action. This review sought the advice and input from people charged with implementing the policies, as well as the ideas of a broad range of stakeholders including members of Congress from both sides of the aisle. Their assessment showed that they could lawfully take action to increase border security, focus enforcement resources, ensure accountability in our immigration system, and provide protections for undocumented youth. These executive actions included:

- Strengthing border security,
- Revising deportation priorities,
- Ending the Secure Communities Program and replacing it with a new Priority Enforcement Program,
- Ensuring personnel reform for Immigration and Customs Enforcement (ICE) officers,
- Expanding DACA,
- Extending Deferred Action to Parents of U.S. Citizens and Lawful Permanent Residents (DAPA),
- Expanding provisional waivers to spouses and children of lawful permanent residents,
- Revising parole rules—parole-in-place and deferred action,
- Revising parole rules—advance parole,
- Promoting the naturalization process, and
- Supporting high-skilled business and workers.

These executive orders worked and provided a roadmap for thoughtful, comprehensive immigration reform that never made it into legislation. However, DACA was Obama's signature order. He used the criteria in the DREAM Act to write the executive order that created DACA. Since the Obama administration launched the program in 2012, eight hundred thousand young people have benefited from it. While DACA does not offer a pathway to legalization, it has moved large numbers of eligible young adults out of the shadows and into the mainstream of our society. As we will see in the next chapter, it has been a wide-ranging success, integrating young adult immigrants into society and providing economic opportunities that were previously unavailable. A recent national survey of undocumented millennials showed that 70 percent say they began their first job or moved to a new job upon receiving DACA, 64 percent say they are less afraid because of their status, and 84 percent now have a driver's license.

Related actions such as Deferred Action to Parents of US Citizens and Lawful Permanent Residents (DAPA) would have provided similar protections to the parents with children born here or ones who had received permanent residency. Together DACA and DAPA would have provided relief to 5.1 million of the estimated 11.1 million undocumented residents of the United States. A federal court in Texas stopped the implementation of DAPA. There was a similar fate for other executive orders such as the Strengthened Border Security Policy that enhanced border enforcement and reduced the number of illegal entries along our southern border and the Secure Communities Program, an ill-conceived program that used local police in immigration enforcement.

I had concerns about DACA back in 2012.[17] My first concern was that undocumented children and youth would continue to live a life of uncertainty with reprieves coming in two-year installments. Second, there was no path to citizenship; undocumented youth would remain in limbo. And third, it was an executive order and not a law, and a future president could rescind the order. My concerns came true on September 5, 2017.

The Trump Administration Rescinds DACA

On September 5, 2017, President Trump through Attorney General Jeff Sessions, announced the cancellation of DACA. Following the announcement, the Department of Homeland Security stopped accepting new DACA applications but would process the DACA requests they had already received. They would also allow participants in the program to continue to renew their applications for a two-year extension if they received renewal requests by October 5th.[18] The six-month delay permitted 24.7 percent of DACA recipients, or 196,510, to renew their permits. The Trump administration would then allow the deferred action of recipients to expire "naturally" at the end of their validity periods. Beginning on March 6, 2018, approximately one thousand recipients per day would lose their deferred action status through March 5, 2020, when the program would end.

There has been a temporary reprieve in this rapidly evolving story. Immediately following the Trump administration's announcement, five lawsuits were filed in US District Court for Northern California to reinstate DACA. On January 9, 2018, District Judge William Alsup ruled,

"Pending final judgment herein or other order, to maintain the DACA program on a nationwide basis on the same terms and conditions that were in effect before the rescission on September 5, 2017." The district court further ordered the federal government to begin renewing work permits for DACA recipients. At the time of this writing, the United States Citizenship and Immigration Services is accepting renewals but not new applications for DACA.[19] However, the DACAmented are still in peril as the appellate process proceeds through the courts.

The administration says that DACA beneficiaries will not become priorities for removal after their permits expire. However, without employment authorization, they will be forced back into the informal job market. More important, Immigration and Customs Enforcement (ICE) announced they will arrest any unauthorized immigrant they encounter. This action would include former DACA recipients it finds during raids targeting their parents.[20]

In his speech on September 5, the attorney general made sweeping generalizations about the nation's immigration, and much of it was untrue. Below are a few examples of his misstatements.

> In other words, the executive branch, through DACA, deliberately sought to achieve what the legislative branch specifically refused to authorize on multiple occasions. Such an open-ended circumvention of immigration laws was an unconstitutional exercise of authority by the Executive Branch.

As we discussed earlier, executive orders have been used by presidents throughout our history to manage the operations of the federal government, and have the force of law.

> The effect of this unilateral executive amnesty, among other things, contributed to a surge of unaccompanied minors on the southern border that yielded terrible humanitarian consequences.

This statement shows a misunderstanding of who is eligible for deportation relief under DACA. The program applies only to immigrants who entered before their sixteenth birthdays and who have lived in the country continuously since at least June 15, 2007. Children who arrived after January 1, 2007, are not eligible. Because of their vulnerability, children who arrive on our border without a parent or guardian receive special protections under US law, but these are not DACA protections. Most of these children come from Central America and cite gang or cartel violence as a primary reason for fleeing, not DACA. Notably, the rise in violence and the corresponding increase in unaccompanied child arrivals precedes the creation of DACA.[21]

> It also denied jobs to hundreds of thousands of Americans by allowing those same jobs to go to illegal aliens.

As we showed in chapter 2, research has consistently demonstrated that immigrants complement rather than compete with US-born workers. This is also true of DACA recipients. United States and immigrant workers have different skill sets and tend to work in different jobs and industries, even when they have similar educational backgrounds.[22] Research on the impact of immigrant labor on wages has similar findings. Immigrants consume goods and services, creating jobs for natives and other immigrants alike thus increasing the average wages of US-born workers by 0.4 percent.[23]

> Enforcing the law saves lives, protects communities and taxpayers, and prevents human suffering

As we saw in chapter 2, first-generation immigrants who enter the United States as children—the population that includes DACA recipients—pay more in taxes over their lifetimes than they receive in benefits, regardless of their education level. DACA recipients contribute more than the average because they are not eligible for federal programs like SNAP (food stamps), Medicaid, and Social Security.[24]

DACA recipients are better educated than the general public. Applicants must have a high school degree to enter the program, and 32 percent are in school pursuing a bachelor's degree. The data show an additional 36 percent of them have a bachelor's degree. Immigrants with a high school degree who entered as children contribute between $60,000 to $153,000 more in their working lives in taxes than they receive in benefits. For those with a bachelor's degree, it is between $160,000 to $316,000.[25]

> Failure to enforce the laws in the past has put our nation at risk of crime, violence and even terrorism.

Wrong again. Unauthorized immigrants—the applicant pool for DACA—are much less likely to be in prison, indicating lower levels of criminality.[26] More important, to participate in DACA, applicants must pass background checks, and only .25 percent of DACA recipients have lost their permits because of public safety concerns.[27]

> That is an open border policy and the American people have rightly rejected it.

We do not have open borders; rather there were several decades when the federal government did not do its job securing our borders. The American people recognize the culpability of our federal government in unauthorized immigration, but true to our national values, they support immigration, current immigration levels, and a path to citizenship for those already here.[28]

The Cost of Rescinding DACA

The Cato Institute is an independent, nonpartisan think tank. In an often-cited article, two of its researchers, Ike Brannon and Logan Albright, explored the cost of President Trump's repeal of DACA.[29] The goal of their research was to estimate the cost the repeal would impose on the American economy in enforcement costs and the sudden loss of hundreds of thousands of workers in the economy. They did not calculate many of the after-effects of such a sudden shift in policy on families, communities, health care, education, the military, the justice system, and other areas of our society.

The authors note that there are no administrative costs for DACA, since applicants cover the expense through an administrative fee. The program requires a background check and screens out anyone with a criminal past. Participants are not eligible for welfare benefits, Medicare, and Social Security, so there are no federal social service costs. Additionally, recipients must have a high school degree or GED and must be enrolled or have received a college degree. At its core, DACA is an education program. As such, participants are not typical immigrants. The average DACA recipient is in her/his twenties, employed, and earning about $17 an hour. The majority are still students, and 17 percent are pursuing a masters, doctorate, or a professional degree. In short, DACA recipients tend to be younger, better educated, and more highly paid than the average immigrant.

A 2014 survey showed that in its first two years, the program had positive effects. Researchers found that 59 percent of DACA recipients reported getting their first job, 45 percent received a pay increase, 49 percent opened their first bank account, and 33 percent received their first credit card. All of these factors contribute positively to the economy. The authors also note that DACA moved between fifty to seventy-five thousand undocumented youth out of the informal cash economy and into the formal labor force where they paid more payroll, income, and sales taxes and, because they had higher incomes, consumed more. There were also savings. Legalizing unauthorized immigrants and allowing them to participate in society dramatically reduced government enforcement costs. They also included in their calculations the cost of deporting DACA recipients, estimated at $7.5 billion

They conclude, "The repeal of DACA would harm the economy and cost the US government a significant amount of lost tax revenue." Furthermore, they estimate that the fiscal cost of immediately deporting the people currently in the DACA program would be more than $60 billion to the federal government along with a $280 billion reduction in economic growth over the next decade. They concluded that any costs of DACA are far "outweighed by the benefits that come from immigrants who are able to work openly and legally, pay taxes, support entitlement programs, create jobs, innovate, and sire children who will one day do the same."

Final Thoughts

Since the beginning of our republic, there has been a concern about the racial and ethnic mix of our society. Our first immigration law in 1790 limited naturalization to immigrants who were "free white persons of good character," and this is a concern found in much of our immigration law. Immigration has been a major domestic issue throughout our history because this process defines who we are and what it means to be an American.

Immigrants are entering an already existing society, and their integration is determined by their racial and ethnic differences from those already here. During the Third Wave of Immigration, Eastern and Southern Europeans and Asians were entering a society defined by Northern and Western European culture. The public met them with hostility, and Congress responded with legislation of exclusion and quotas. Beginning in the 1970s, immigrants from the Americas and Asia began entering a society that was 88 percent white, and the Fourth Wave of Immigration has received a similar welcome. Much of the immigration legislation over the past third of a century has had the same racial undertones, and this is true of the DREAM Act and DACA.

Perhaps the most ill-advised immigration policy of the Trump administration has been the termination of DACA. Ending DACA forces young immigrants back into the shadows because they face deportation. Thrust into the informal labor market because they can no longer work legally, they earn less, buy less, pay fewer taxes, and lose the protections of labor laws. DACA has been an unqualified success and has benefited not only the DACA recipients but also our nation and its economy. In the next chapter, we explore the economic, political, and social impact of this program.

FOUR

DACA by the Numbers

A Successful Policy, a Costly End

> I was shocked; my heart was pounding, I wondered if I had wandered off into an alternate universe where it was possible to dare think that I might have a real shot at getting papers.
>
> A friend called me when I got to my office and congratulated me, and I had no idea why. When I found out, I just went crazy and started pulling up every online article I could and posting them on Facebook, calling up my brother, my sister, my undergrad adviser. . . . It was a very happy morning. I watched the official announcement from the White House later that day and shared my story with some of the other students in my office for the first time. I was very relieved to hear that they supported a policy like this.
>
> It changes my outlook and plans. I have some real hope of being able to get my Ph.D. in this country now. . . . I had really dreaded the prospect of leaving. I'm looking forward to getting my driver's license and being able to be a teaching assistant.[1]

I received this e-mail from Jazmin a few hours after President Obama's July 15, 2012, bombshell announcement that deportation rules would be eased to allow some young undocumented immigrants to remain in the United States. Jazmin, like many of her fellow Dreamers, received the news with a mixture of joy, relief, hope, disbelief, caution, and distrust.

Presidential Obama created DACA through executive action, a presidential power based on the principle of administrative discretion. As we learned in the last chapter, presidents, governors, judges, and department heads have limited resources to address problems, so they are permitted by law to make discretionary decisions in the discharge of their public duties as long as another branch of government reviews them. The thinking of the Obama administration was that it made little sense to expend time and resources trying to track down, arrest, and deport these young people when they had committed no crime. Others brought them to this country, and as minors, they had no agency in the decision to break the law. The administration felt government's resources could be better used to arrest and deport criminals, and the Obama administration deported a record number of unauthorized immigrants, many of them felons.[2]

The Trump administration has taken an absolutist position on all immigration policies, vowing to build a wall to reduce illegal entry across the Mexican-US border, ending visas for family reunification, halting the green card lottery system, and halving the number of visas for highly skilled workers. On September 5, 2017, President Trump signed an executive order to nullify President Obama's executive actions dealing with immigration, including the one that created DACA. As with any drastic policy shifts, there are costs associated with its implementation, as well as unintended consequences that won't come to light immediately.

This chapter examines DACA through a series of questions. How many were eligible for DACA and how many were granted relief by US Immigration and Citizenship Immigration Services? Who are they? Where do they live? What are they doing? Think tanks have evaluated the success of DACA. What did they find? Are the DACAmented integrating into the fabric of our communities and society? What are the costs of ending the program? How many young people face deportation?

Eligible, Applied, and Granted DACA

In the last chapter, we reviewed DACA and learned that applicants must have entered the United States before age sixteen, lived in the country continuously since June 2007, met educational requirements, committed no serious crimes, and passed a background check to be awarded DACA. Since its repeal, the media have reported numbers of recipients from a low of 580,000 to a high of nearly 800,000 at risk of losing their deferment. The president recently announced that he would support a bill that would provide relief to 1.8 million eligible undocumented youth. So, what are the right numbers?

The Pew Research Center estimates that about 1.1 million unauthorized immigrants were eligible for DACA and 78 percent of them applied to the program. This total reflects the number of applications during the life of the program, not the number of applications approved or immigrants currently receiving benefits.[3] Approximately eight hundred thousand young unauthorized immigrants received work permits and protection from deportation through DACA since the program's inception in 2012. As of September 4, 2017, 689,000 unauthorized youth were still enrolled in the program.[4] Approximately 110,000 recipients have dropped out—seventy thousand DACA participants did not renew their benefits or had their renewal applications denied; forty thousand changed their legal status, obtained green cards or asylum, obtained legal status by marrying an American citizen or lawful permanent resident, or received other types of visas.[5]

Congress is weighing legislation to give Dreamers a chance to stay legally in the United States. At the time of this writing in February 2018, senators from both sides of the aisle had filed five DREAM Act-like bills—American Hope Act, Border Security and Deferred Action Recipient Relief Act, DREAM Act of 2017, Recognizing America's Children Act, and SUCCEED Act.

The proposed legislation differ on three criteria that applicants need to be eligible for relief: (1) meeting the minimum age at arrival and years of US residence; (2) achieving educational and other requirements to gain conditional permanent residency; and (3) fulfilling post-secondary education, military service, or employment requirements that allow legal permanent residence (green cards) and a path to citizenship.[6] It is a three-stage process. Applicants must qualify in stage 1 to proceed to stage 2 before being awarded permanent legal status in stage 3. The number of those eligible declines as they move through the process.

Table 4.1 shows the Migration Policy Institute's estimates of potential beneficiaries under each legislative proposal. Note that the numbers of undocumented youth receiving relief differs dramatically across the bills. For example, the size of the initial pool of applicants meeting

Table 4.1. Estimating the Unauthorized Populations that Could Benefit Under Differen Legalization Bills in Congress

	RAC Act	DREAM Act of 2017	American Hope Act	SUCCEED Act	Border Security and Deferred Action Recipient Relief Act
Meet minimum threshold based on initial age at arrival and length of US residence criteria	2,408,000	3,245,000	3,571,000	2,035,000	2,408,000
Eligible for conditional permanent resident status	1,751,000	2,139,000	3,571,000	1,587,000	1,751,000
Eligible for legal permanent resident status	1,399,000	1,730,000	3,571,000	1,253,000	1,399,000

Source: Batalova, Jeanne, Ariel B. Ruiz Soto, Sarah Pierce, and Randy Capps. 2017. "Differing Dreams: Estimating the Unauthorized Populations that could Benefit under Different Legalization Bills," Migration Policy Institute, https://www.migrationpolicy.org/research/differing-dreams-estimating-unauthorized-populations-could-benefit-under-different, accessed December 18, 2018.

the age and residency requirement ranges from a high of 3.6 million in the American Hope Act to a low of 2 million in the SUCCEED Act. Similarly, the pool of those eligible to apply for legal permanent residence with a path to citizenship varies from a high of 3.6 million to a low of 1.3 million in these same bills.[7] If a legislative solution is found in the Senate and the bill makes it to the floor of the House, these bills will provide the framework for the compromise.

Who Are They? What Are They Doing? Where Do They Live?

The Migration Policy Institute (MPI) and the Pew Research Center are independent, nonpartisan, nonprofit think tanks in Washington, DC. I find them an indispensable source of reliable data on immigration issues. The US Citizenship and Immigration Services (USCIS) released new data in fall 2017, the most extensive ever. Using these data, the centers published a series of reports that provided a profile of DACA participants. These are their findings.

DACA participants averaged 6.5 years old when they first arrived in the United States, and two-thirds of them are twenty-five or younger. Women make up a slight majority (53 percent). The average age of DACA enrollees is twenty-four, and those twenty-five and younger make up two-thirds of active recipients. Most current DACA recipients (83 percent) are unmarried.[8]

The overwhelming majority of DACA participants are Hispanic (92.8 percent) and nearly 80 percent of them are from Mexico. Although the vast majority of recipients are from Latin America, USCIS data show that youth from more than two hundred countries have received relief through the program.[9]

Forty-five percent of recipients are currently in school, and of those in school, 72 percent are pursuing a bachelor's degree or higher. Twenty-eighty percent already hold a bachelor's degree.

Often ignored in the immigration debate is that most DACA recipients live in a mixed-status household—73 percent have parents, siblings, spouses, and children who are US citizens or legal permanent residents, and 45 percent of these are eighteen years old or older. Therefore, deporting a DACA youth would disrupt families, kin networks, and communities. There would be political consequences too—an overwhelming percentage (81 percent) of immediate family members who are US citizens are registered to vote.[10]

Using these same data, the MPI compiled an employment profile of recipients. DACA participants are largely middle-skilled, either enrolled in school, or working, or both. The analysis shows that DACA recipients work across a wide range of industries and occupations, and are integrated into many different parts of the nation's economy. Although they have become a symbol of a flawed immigration system, they account for a minuscule part of the workforce, .25 percent.[11]

- Sixty-four percent are in the labor force and 55 percent are working, accounting for 382,000 workers. Eight percent are unemployed.
- One-out-of three DACA recipients is enrolled in school and also works—a rate roughly the same as the general population of the same age.
- DACA holders are more likely to work in office support jobs compared to undocumented youth without DACA who tend to work in construction. These data show that DACA contributes to occupational mobility.
- A significant number of DACA recipients are employed in professional occupations.
- The most common industries of employment for DACA recipients are hospitality, retail trade, construction, education, health and social services, and professional services. Nine thousand work in arts, entertainment and food services; fifty-four thousand in retail; fourteen thousand in real estate or financial services; nine thousand are teachers or education professionals; and fourteen thousand are in health-care practitioner or support jobs.

Where do they live?

Nine out of ten were born in Latin America, but DACA recipients come from around the world, and most arrived in the historic immigrant gateway cities of San Francisco, Los Angeles, San Diego, Houston, Dallas, Miami, New York City, and Chicago. Three-quarters of DACA recipients live in just twenty metropolitan areas. With eighty-

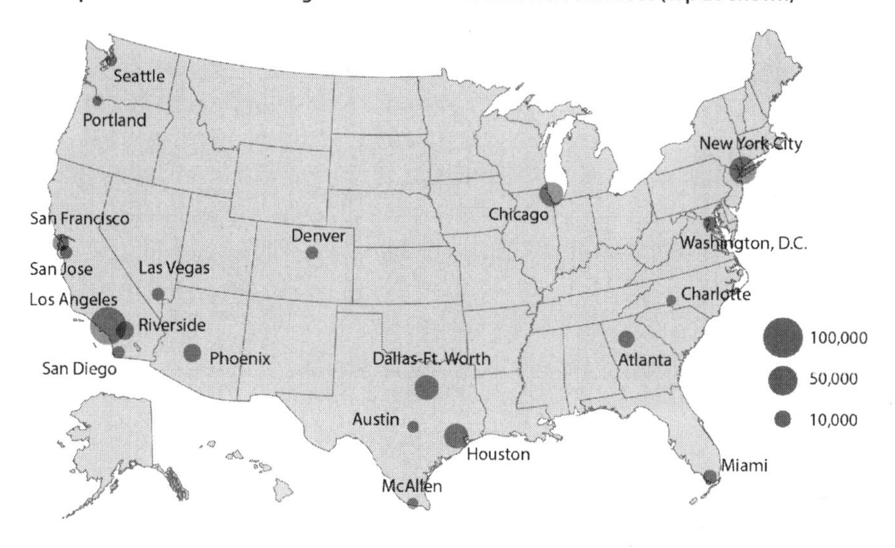

Note: Only refers to individuals who are active DACA recipients, as of September 4, 2017.

Figure 4.1

"Where 'Dreamers' Enrolled in DACA Lived in 2017."

Source: López, Gustavo and Jens Manuel Krogstad. 2017. "Key Facts about Unauthorized Immigrants Enrolled in DACA. Pew Research Center: Pew Research Center," Pew Research Center, http://www.pewresearch.org/fact-tank/2017/09/25/key-facts-about-unauthorized-immigrants-enrolled-in-daca/, accessed December 18, 2017.

nine thousand recipients, Los Angeles had the largest number of active enrollees on September 5, 2017, followed by Dallas, Houston, and New York City. More than 60 percent of the recipients live in just six states: California (29 percent), Texas (16 percent), Illinois (five percent), New York (five percent), Florida (four percent), and Arizona (four percent). Although the media have framed DACA as a national issue, only a handful of states were highly affected by DACA's rescission.[12]

How are they doing?

In August 2017, Tom K. Wong of the University of California, San Diego conducted a national survey to analyze further the economic, employment, educational, and societal experiences of DACA recipients.

This survey was his most recent in a series of surveys that documented the experiences of DACA participants.[13]

Professor Wong's data illustrated the significant impact the program has had on the recipients' economic well-being, education, and social integration. For example, work authorization was a critical part of DACA because it allowed participants to move out of the informal labor market into a legal one that provides benefits and labor law protections. Wong's data show that only 44 percent of respondents were employed before DACA. Ninety-one percent are currently employed, and among respondents age twenty-five and older, employment jumps to 93 percent. DACA recipients also reported the following improvements in their financial well-being.

- The average hourly wage of respondents increased nearly 70 percent after receiving DACA, rising from $10.29 to $17.46 per hour. Among respondents older than twenty-five, the wage increase was 84 percent. Calculated as annual earnings, incomes jumped to an average of $36,232. For those twenty-five and older, the figure rose to $41,621.
- More than half reported finding a job that better fits their education and long-term career goals, had improved working conditions, or jobs that provided health insurance and other benefits.
- More than 60 percent reported they opened their first bank account, secured their first credit card, and two-thirds bought their first car. Sixteen percent of the respondents bought their first home. Among respondents older than twenty-five, this percentage was 24 percent.
- More than 70 percent reported earning enough money to live independently and said they were able to increase financial assistance to their families.

Research done by others shows that DACA beneficiaries tend to be employed in higher-skilled jobs than other unauthorized workers. Seventy-two percent of the top twenty-five Fortune 500 companies employ DACA recipients. Since they are better educated than the general immigrant population, they have the capacity to make significantly more money over their working lives and make our economy more productive.[14]

Other findings pointed to greater inclusion and belonging. For example, 80 percent obtained a driver's license for the first time, 55 percent qualified for a state identification card, and nearly half became organ donors.

Living in the shadows takes a psychological toll. The most heartening findings from other surveys of DACA recipients are their improved health and mental well-being. DACA recipients are more likely than nonrecipients to have health insurance and fewer reported delaying necessary medical care during the past twelve months. Psychological well-being? DACA recipients are less likely to report indicators of stress (nervousness or anxiety) compared to nonrecipients. Similarly, DACA recipients were also less likely to report feeling sadness, embarrassment, or shame than nonrecipients, and were four times less likely to report worry about being arrested or deported than nonrecipients. But regardless of DACA status, respondents with or without DACA reported worry about family members being arrested or deported. Their fears are real: a majority of respondents knew someone who had been deported and more than half reported that a family member had been deported.[15]

These studies show that DACA has had a significant impact on the economic and psychological well-being, education, and social integration of recipients. Fully participating in society allows them to increase earning, saving, and consumption, as well as pay more taxes and contribute to the Social Security and Medicare Trust Funds—contributions to an economy that benefit all Americans. More important, removing the threat of deportation has reduced their anxiety, depression, and fear, an outcome that all Americans should celebrate for these young people.

How DACA Will End

There were three parts to DACA outlined in Secretary Janet Napolitano's June 15, 2012, memorandum that created the program. First, the secretary of the Department Homeland Security (DHS) deprioritized the removal of noncriminal unauthorized immigrants and directed its agents to prevent Dreamers that they encounter "from being placed into removal proceedings or removed from the United States." Second, it established a program whereby recipients would have removal action against them "deferred" for two years. DHS reclassified them as "lawfully present." Finally, DACA authorized the immigrants to receive an employment authorization document (EAD) that was valid for two years; they could legally seek employment.[16]

President Trump's September 5, 2017, executive order ended the deportation protections and work authorization beginning on March 5, 2018. Under the new guidelines, immigrants holding DACA permits expiring between September 5, 2017, and March 5, 2018, could apply for a two-year renewal until October 5, 2017. However, a federal court injunction in January 2018 meant that the Trump administration must keep DACA in place for now. The US Citizenship and Immigration Services is once again accepting renewals.

On January 9, 2018, in *Regents of the University of California* v. *Department of Homeland Security*, a federal judge issued a temporary order directing the government to reinstate DACA on a nationwide basis on the same terms and conditions as were in effect before its rescission on September 5, 2017. It is a temporary reprieve as the case works its way to the US Supreme Court. But what happens if the plaintiff loses the appeal? The MPI estimates, published days after the September 5th announcement, that an average of 915 young unauthorized immigrants per day would lose their work authorization and protection from deportation beginning on March 6, 2018, through March 5, 2020. The expirations would have peaked in January through March 2019, when approximately fifty thousand individuals would lose their DACA protections each month. Annually, a total of 201,678 permits would expire in 2018, another 275,344 in 2019, and 321,920 would expire from January through August 2020. Once permits expire, former DACA recipients will no longer be eligible to work legally and will face deportation.[17] If the executive order is upheld and Congress fails to pass immigration legislation, the numbers will be the same, only the start dates will differ.

Will there be a mass deportation of DACA recipients when the court injunction expires? DHS says it's not going to change the way it prioritizes its deportations—felons would still be the top priority.[18] But less is known about the agency that enforces our immigration laws—Immigration and Customs Enforcement (ICE). Will they change their policies? For example, will they deport former DACA beneficiaries if they are caught up in a sweep of a neighborhood, shopping area, or business? A recent internal memorandum that I received suggests harsher deportation policies are being put in place by the agency.[19]

The question remains whether or not Congress will pass a bill and finally deliver on the comprehensive immigration reform people have been waiting on for decades. Other questions are, under what conditions will House majority Republicans agree to protect the Dreamers? Will future legal immigrants and present immigrants bear the brunt of their actions? What compromises is Congress willing to accept to save the Dreamers?

The Economic Costs of Ending DACA

DACA recipients are low-cost citizens. They funded the deferred action program with their application fees. They cannot collect welfare benefits. They pay federal, state, and local taxes, and contribute to the Social Security and Medicare Trust Funds from which they can receive no benefits. They live in limbo with an immigration status of "lawfully present," and in return, they get work authorization and a deportation reprieve in two-year installments. What are the costs of ending DACA?

We have shown the program has been successful, especially in the economic well-being of DACA recipients. Nearly 91 percent of them are working, earning a combined $30 billion a year. The most apparent impact of ending DACA is the abrupt exit of hundreds of thousands of workers from the labor market, a change that will have a ripple effect on the economy.

Economists use a tool called the "multiplier-effect" to estimate the direct and indirect benefits from a policy. When DACA participants rent or buy a home, and buy groceries, clothes, and automobiles, they create demand. To meet the new demand, businesses hire more workers and this creates a virtuous cycle that benefits us all. A multiplier of $1 of earnings to $7 in economic benefit is standard, and applying it to the US economy would theoretically represent a $210 billion per year loss. But most DACA recipients will move into the underground economy when they lose their legal jobs and receive 10 to 20 percent less pay and no benefits. The resulting economic impact is estimated to be around $40 to 45 billion per year, not an insubstantial sum. Therefore, the estimated cost of ending DACA would be a loss of $460.3 billion from the national GDP over the next decade.[20] There are other costs as well. Replacement and retraining costs for businesses forced to hire new workers because of the loss of trained DACA workers is estimated at $6.5 billion. Deportation costs per person is near $10,000 per removal, and in a worst-case scenario, they represent $7.5 billion.[21] Contributions to the Social Security and Medicare Trust Funds would decline by $39.3 billion over ten years.[22] And the disruption of the networks of families, friends, and communities is incalculable.

Most of the nation's immigration debate has focused on national policies, and their impact on California, Texas, Florida, Arizona, and other states with large immigrant populations. But other states and regions have a lot at stake as well.[23] A recent report by the Brookings Institute focused on the consequences of ending DACA in the Midwest. It's called the Rust Belt for a reason—it has been losing population and businesses to other regions of the country for decades. With a rapidly aging workforce, immigrants are the region's major source of population and business growth. Ending DACA will remove nearly fifty thousand people from the workforce with a loss of $2.8 billion in the region's economy. The Rust Belt's efforts to transform itself into a knowledge- and information-based economy would be undercut by the loss of Dreamers, who tend to be better educated than the general immigrant community[24]

I have focused on the economic, social, and psychological costs of ending DACA. A recent Twitter feed by former Mexican president Vicente Fox summed up many of the most underappreciated costs of ending the program—the loss of human capital. He said:

> If you don't want DACA here, we'll take all of them in Mexico. We would love to have them in Mexico. I mean, imagine kids with a university degree, with the knowledge that very few have, with the capacities and skills they have developed in themselves. We would love to have them in Mexico, but we respect their will

> to be in the United States. We respect that they love their families and they want to stay. But if not, please DACA, come here. Come back to Mexico. We will have a future for you there.[25]

The US Department of Agriculture estimates that families can expect to spend between between $174,690 and $372,210 to raise a child through high school. Add college expenses, and this figure goes up by tens of thousands of dollars.[26] These are family expenses. The numbers do not include public expenditures for education, health care, and the range of services provided by all communities—fire, police, parks and recreation, roads to name a few. These costs represent this society's investment in our human capital, our most important asset. Our nation's potential, its future, is tied to the education, skills, and talents of our people.

What Americans seldom appreciate is that migration represents the transfer of these investments from one society to another. Decades of research show that people who migrate for economic opportunities are different from those who stay behind. They tend to be better educated, more ambitious and entrepreneurial, and are willing to take the risks and assume the costs for a better future in a new society. They pass these qualities onto their children. Therefore, the countries of origin of our forty-three million immigrants have watched their investments benefit us. This is especially true when they are highly educated and skilled. Their economies are less prosperous; ours is more. Mexico, in particular, has transferred billions of dollars of its wealth to the United States over the past forty years. President Fox's words should resonate with Americans, "(I)magine kids with a university degree, with the knowledge that very few have, with the capacities and skills they have developed in themselves. We would love to have them in Mexico." Imagine what our country can be if we tap the potential of these undocumented youth in our society.

FIVE

Allies

Four People Making a Difference

Setting: The Office of the Arkansas United Community Coalition

Springdale, Arkansas, September 5, 2017, 5:30 PM

The Trump administration had announced the rescission of DACA that morning. Mireya Reith, the director of the Arkansas United Community Coalition (AUCC), hastily called a meeting that evening. AUCC was ready; they had contingency plans in place for the worst.

The tension was palpable when my wife and I walked into the AUCC offices. I looked over the packed room and saw a lot of familiar faces. Many in the room were Dreamers whom I had known since they were teens. They weren't teens anymore, but adults with husbands and wives and, in a few cases, children. Univision and the local Fox Affiliate had set up the cameras. Seated at a table in the front was Frank Head, the director of Catholic Immigration Services; Christina Pollard, a lawyer with the University of Arkansas Immigration Legal Clinic; and Laura Ferner, a local immigration attorney. My eyes briefly met those of Juan Mendez, the founder of Arkansas Natural Dreamers, who gave me a grim smile.

Mireya introduced the panel, and they each took turns giving their analysis of the day's events and what they thought was in the future. Then there were questions and answers. What were the politics behind the rescission of DACA? Would they have the opportunity to renew their deferments? Should they? When would protections end? What was the timeline for the phase-out? Were there alternative strategies for gaining temporary legal status? Would Immigration and Customs Enforcement (ICE) use the personal information on their DACA application to arrest them? Would ICE ramp up the area's enforcement? What should they do if they got caught up in a traffic stop or an ICE sweep in their neighborhood, workplace, home, or grocery? If arrested, what were the chances ICE would deport them? But the most gut-wrenching questions came later as the crowd broke up into smaller groups.

As I walked around the room, I heard parents talk about other fears. They wondered what would happen to their children if they were deported? Should their first- and second-graders start carrying cell phones to school, so they could be notified if their parents had been arrested? Should they sign a power of attorney and custody directives to friends and relatives so that someone could care for their children if they were gone? As the evening wore on, the conversations were increasingly filled with words of despair. Their lives as they had known them were coming to an end. In the months ahead, they would be losing their jobs and security as they moved back into the shadows. Frank Head, a long-time immigration advocate, ended the meeting by saying, "I am ashamed to be an American today. This is not who we are." Everyone present seemed to agree.

Something else happened that night. As I looked around the room, I noticed that there weren't just the undocumented in the room, but also many allies of the Dreamers—the Frank Heads and the Laura Ferners in this community. They were there that night because they were deeply troubled by what was happening in our community. And they were quietly working in the background, investing their time, money, and careers in bringing about change. In this chapter, I highlight the contributions of four of them.

For the past twenty years, Jeanette Arnhart has taught Spanish for Native Speakers in the Rogers and Springdale Public Schools and at the University of Arkansas. She is a passionate advocate for immigrant youth, with a unique insight into the daily challenges facing her immigrant students and their families.

Laura Ferner is a native of Germany, an immigrant who knows the immigration and naturalization process firsthand. She has a general immigration law practice, serves on the board of AUCC, and brings a special perspective to this chapter on the legal challenges facing the undocumented and DACA participants.

Mireya Reith is the director and cofounder of the AUCC—a nonprofit dedicated to empowering immigrants through leadership development, coalition building, advocacy, the promotion of civic engagement, and immigration service navigation. She currently serves on the Board of the Arkansas Department of Education, where she represents the interest of the state's immigrant students. There is no one I know who knows more about immigration politics in Arkansas.

Luis Restrepo joined the University of Arkansas faculty in 1995, and is the current director of the Comparative Literature and Cultural Studies Program. We serve together on the board of EngageNWA, a nonprofit working to speed the integration of immigrants into the fabric of our community. In 2011, he established Sin Limites, the Latino Youth Biliteracy Project, a service-learning initiative involving upper-level Spanish students mentoring elementary- and middle- school Spanish heritage speakers. He has also served at the university as the assistant vice chancellor for diversity and community and founded La Oficina Latina—the Office of Latino Academic Advancement and Community Relations. He has broad insights into challenges facing DACAmented college students.

In fall 2017, I led a documentary-film class, "DACA: The Arkansas Latino Experience," at the David and Barbara Pryor Center for Oral and Visual History.[1] During this turbulent time in our nation's immigration history, my students, and I wanted to focus on undocumented youth. We videotaped DACAmented youth, authorized immigrants, students, teachers, professors, immigration professionals, activists, and opponents of immigration reform. My students are using the interviews to create a documentary this spring (2018). Some of their interviews provided the material for this chapter.

Jeanette Arnhart

In 2007, I conducted a year-long study of the region's Hispanic community for the Walton Family Foundation. Our six-member team interviewed more than one hundred people, conducted more than a dozen focus groups, and completed a content analysis of the region's English

Figure 5.1
Jeanette A. Arnhart with her student at Lakeside Jr. High School, Springdale, Arkansas. Photograph by Ashley LeAnn Miller.

and Spanish-language newspapers. We learned a lot about the characteristics and needs of this community.

I met Jeanette while leading a focus group of English as a Second Language teachers in the Rogers, Arkansas, School District. She stood out. I was impressed with her use of cutting-edge pedagogy, her deep understanding of the challenges facing her students and their families, her work with them in and outside the classroom, and her caring and understanding of the challenges they faced. I soon learned of the Hispanic Community's respect for Dr. Arnhart.

We have kept in touch. I've attended some of the events she organized for her students, and I have watched her on panels discussing the plight of undocumented students. As a doctoral student, she helped shape the University of Arkansas's outreach to the region's immigrant community. I interviewed her for my last book, *The Right to DREAM*. I've turned to her again in writing this book because of her vast knowledge of our community and because she is an ally of the Dreamers and the DACAmented. My students' first interview was with Jeanette on September 23, 2017, eighteen days after the rescission of DACA.

Jeanette has taught Spanish for Native Speakers since 1999. She describes herself as an ally of the undocumented. Her commitment to her students and her advocacy reverberated throughout the interview. She opened by saying:

> As a teacher, I have to stand up for them. Sometimes standing in front of them. Sometimes standing behind them. Doing whatever it is that I have to do. I have marched with students in Washington. I have marched with them in Northwest Arkansas, Dallas, Kansas City, and Little Rock. I have written many, many letters of support for parents. I do anything I can do to help them succeed and help them be proud of who they are. Help them understand that it is not their fault and that they deserve an education. Understand they deserve a home. That this is their home. . . . How can we deny them the fullness of being a citizen?

When asked, "How has DACA affected your students?" Jeanette described her students before and after DACA. She started by giving a history of our region. She told us that it was the early 2000s when most of the Latino population came to Northwest Arkansas and had their first impact on the region's schools. She described the undocumented students as a complex mix coming from Los Angeles, Houston, and several states in Mexico. Most of the male students came to work in local chicken processing plants and didn't know they were supposed to go to school. She said, "We ran the gamut from those who couldn't read and write to those who were educated to fifth, sixth, or seventh grade in their countries."

She described her role, at first, as helping them feel as if they belonged and teaching them about the district's educational system. Her role soon grew to helping them face the daunting challenges of learning English, a new culture, a new education system, and new social norms. Later, when she heard her students say, "Why try? Why put out my best effort? Why dream when the dream will be taken way? Jeanette worked "to instill a sense of hope, to motivate them to strive to fulfill their potential, starting with a high school degree."

We asked Jeanette, to describe what it was like for her students before DACA. Before DACA, the idea of attending college or getting a real job wasn't even on her students' radar, and it was painful for her to listen to them talk about college. "They would lower their eyes because they had no right and no way to be able to go to school. To be able to get a real job. To be able to get a home. To be successful." Since DACA, these same students had come to believe that anything is possible. The program is working as hoped. She described their successes:

> We have students with DACA who have their masters and doctorate degrees, who are employed by some of the world's largest corporations, leading civil organizations, and working in our health clinics. . . . DACA recipients are in every aspect of our community's life now. They own businesses, they work hard, they are marrying, they are having children, and they are building a life in Northwest Arkansas. And they are becoming pillars of our community. . . . They are what an American is supposed to be. They are not asking for handouts. They are not asking for anything. They are just asking to stay. To live their lives fully.

What is happening to them now that DACA has ended? Many of her former students are in their twenties and early thirties and have built a life here. They are angry because they have to go back to square one and start again. They are angry because they have to relive a painful part of their lives that they thought was over. She is angry because she is watching her former students lose the life that they worked so hard to attain.

Many opponents of immigration reform argue that this newest wave of immigrants is not integrating into the fabric of our communities. Our interviews with Jeanette and others refute this claim. She described the weddings and graduations of her former students, and the change in these celebrations she has seen over the past twenty years. She thinks there is a new dynamic in our community. In the past, "Salvadorans stayed with Salvadorans, Mexicans stayed with Mexicans, and the poor Guatemalans were in between . . . and the Anglo kids just stayed in their area." Not anymore. These young adults grew up together and are bringing down barriers. "These people are truly doing what the American Dream is supposed to be. . . . Only these kids are doing better because they are fully bilingual, biliterate, and bicultural, and they're able to reach out to everyone." In her opinion, without DACA this change might not have happened.

Toward the end of the interview, we asked: "So what do you tell your students about the end of DACA?" She reflected for a moment. "You know as a teacher, as an adult, they look to me for answers. I know what is morally correct, and I know what is right, but I don't have an answer. The only answer that I can give them is that to my dying day I will be beside you. I will fight for you. I will work with you. We will not stop." She talked about activism—marching, writing letters, calling politicians, and electing officials who will do right by our children. Surprisingly she is optimistic. She thinks the rescission of DACA has awakened people. It has started a conversation that wasn't there before. People who were quiet in the past are standing up and becoming involved. And she thinks our elected officials will do the right thing because if they don't, advocates and allies will vote them out of office. This spirit is a testament to the need and importance of allies like Jeanette Arnhart.

Laura K. Ferner

Laura K. Ferner is an immigration attorney with a general practice in Springdale, Arkansas. The home of Tyson Foods, Springdale has always been a blue-collar city. Until the 1970s, it was all white with a "sundown ordinance" that required people of color to be out of town after dark. How things have changed in the past fifty years! Springdale, with a population of eighty thousand, has the region's most diverse ethnic populations including Hmong, Vietnamese, Cambodians, and Laotians. Ten thousand Marshallese call it home, as do twenty-five thousand residents of Hispanic origin.

Laura is fascinating. She was raised in Heidelberg, Germany, where her father was an attorney who specialized in asylum cases, and both of her parents had a passion for social justice. Laura said, "They were always demonstrating for something—ending nuclear power, apartheid." She also went to an international school with sixty nationalities, and her school taught her an important lesson— "the world is a big place, and we should get along." She was like many of her generation:

Figure 5.2
Immigration Lawyer Laura K. Ferner in her law office, Springdale, Arkansas. ©2018 University Relations.

she went to law school because she didn't know what she wanted to do after college. Once there, she took a course in immigration law from Roy Petty, a local attorney, and fell in love with the field and found her life's calling.

Laura explained that immigration law is a complex field with her clients having a full range of legal issues. Initially, she had few undocumented youths as clients, but that changed in June 2012, with the Obama administration's announcement of Deferred Action for Childhood Arrivals. Her DACA clients range from ages fifteen to thirty. The majority have renewed their deferments several times, but some did not return this time because of the uncertainty about the program. Most of her clients are students enrolled in undergraduate or graduate courses at a nearby college or university with the youngest attending one of the area high schools. DACAmented students pay out-of-state or international tuition, so their degrees typically take longer, but she noted they are moving into good jobs after graduation.

Laura's description of the impact of DACA on the lives of her clients mirrored Jeanette's. "DACA gave them a sense of hope, excitement, and plans for a future that they didn't think possible." Her clients work in every sector of the region's economy including some for the Fortune 500 companies located in the area. She also described how the DACAmented have opened businesses, bought homes, married, had children, and created a life here. But she also explained the unique challenges many of them face because of their status. One teenager had just finished his cancer treatment. Ineligible for the Affordable Care Act, he is alive because he was able to get treatment at the Arkansas Children's Hospital in Little Rock. Another wants to join the military, but cannot, even with Legal Permanent Residency (LPR) status, because of recent policy changes made by the Trump administration.

We asked, "What is going to happen with the end of DACA?" She said, "Unauthorized parents came here to give their kids a better life. These people are unauthorized, not criminals. They are not felons. They broke a civil law like speeding or jaywalking." And as an attorney, her primary concern is that the rescission of DACA criminalizes youth and puts them in peril for deportation. She points out that they gave their personal information to US Citizenship and Immigration Services (USCIS) in their application, and she worries that it will be used against them and their parents. Of equal concern is the emotional roller coaster the DACAmented have been riding because of the extreme uncertainty of their futures. All they have garnered from politicians are false hopes and promises that there will be a permanent fix.

Laura sees little hope of congressional action. She noted, "DACA came about because Congress couldn't get its act together." When asked, "What should Congress do?" She said, "Talk to an immigration attorney. Few politicians know current law and the problems immigration attorneys face." And she gave an example. "A Mexican father, who is a US citizen, wants to apply for a visa for his children, but if they have turned twenty-one, they have to wait twenty years to apply. If they get married and have children they can never apply. This is something that could be easily fixed if members of Congress ever talked to an immigration attorney." She reviewed several of the bills that were under consideration in the Senate such as The Reforming American Immigration for Strong Employment (RAISE) Act sponsored by Senator Tom Cotton (R-Arkansas). The bill proposes granting LPR status (a green card) but not citizenship. In Laura's mind, "The bill would create second-class citizens." It would also end the visa program for family reunification. She wondered, "Is denying family reunification, so-called chain-migration, unconstitutional?" Children born in the United States can't apply for their parents' visas? Her concern is Congress will pass a law that will just make things worse.

At the end of her interview, she shared that immigration lawyers are in the trenches and see an enormous array of clients. They tend to be advocates. Laura, for example, is on the board of AUCC, she represents the undocumented, and she uses the courts to challenge policies she feels are unconstitutional. But her advice for the rest of us is: "Get the word out. Get more people to know about the problem. Care about the cause. Get involved and understand the process. If you have the passion, invest your time and money."

Mireya Reith

Mireya Reith is the executive director and cofounder of the Arkansas United Community Coalition (AUCC), an advocacy organization for immigrant rights. Incorporated in 2010 and fully operational since January 2012, the organization has helped twenty thousand immigrants register to vote and four hundred to apply for citizenship. The AUCC is a coalition of several nonprofits that help immigrants develop their leadership potential. Mireya says that the organization's goal is to empower immigrants through leadership development and to give them "the chance to grow by taking on projects meaningful to them and their communities." The organization also works with the DACAmented advocating for immigration reform and an Arkansas DREAM Act that would provide in-state tuition for undocumented youth.

A graduate of Fayetteville High School, she earned degrees from Williams College, Williamstown, MA and Columbia University. After college, she pursued a fourteen-year career in international development, working on projects around the world. Upon returning to Fayetteville, she began volunteering, and was drawn to immigra-

Figure 5.3
Mireya Reith, the director of the Arkansas United Community Coalition (AUCC).

tion issues because of her international experience and her family. Her mother is from Mexico and Mireya describes herself as a Mexican immigrant. Students interviewed Mireya in her AUCC office on September 26, 2017.

Mireya's work in immigration advocacy began in 2010 when Arkansas's two senators, Blanche Lincoln and Mark Pryor, voted against the DREAM Act. The bill had already passed the House, and if Senate Democrats had voted together, the bill would have become law with only one Republican vote. A few years earlier, Arkansas changed its policy on in-state tuition. Until then, an undocumented student didn't need a Social Security number to apply for in-state tuition, only proof that she/he had graduated from an Arkansas high school. Consequently, Arkansas Dreamers who already could not become citizens, faced deportation, worked in the low-paying informal economy, now were priced out of college with out-of-state tuition. The undocumented needed an advocate, and Mireya was just the right person.

Arkansas has a population of three million, and only five percent of its population is foreign born, compared to 13 percent of the US population. Although this population is relatively small, the state ranked fourth nationally in the growth rate of its foreign-born population. Two-thirds of state's immigrants are from Latin America, half from Mexico, and more than 40 percent are unauthorized. In her interview, Mireya described other ways the character of the state's immigration population makes her work more challenging. "This is a rural state, and sixty percent of our immigrants live in communities of eight thousand or less. It is a problem organizing a dispersed population; it is easier in urban places. Arkansas is not only rural, it is conservative, and organizing and activism are viewed negatively in the state and its small communities." She also pointed out that the Northwest Arkansas metro area has the largest immigrant population in the state, and it is "mixed and diverse, with the majority coming to the region for work in the chicken industry, construction, day labor, and service jobs." You can see the impact of the immigrants across our region, but it is most visible in our schools where some already have student bodies with a majority of minority students.

Our interview turned to DACA, and we asked her, "What was it like before deferred action?" Her description echoed Jeanette and Laura's.

> There was uncertainty, fear, and frustration, and the region's undocumented males had the worst high school graduation rates in the state. As we reported earlier, many undocumented youths discovered they were unauthorized when they tried to get a driver's license or began applying to college. They also learned that without a Social Security number they'd be paying out-of-state tuition. She used the word *despair* to describe the mental state of these young people. As did Jeanette and Laura, she would often hear the undocumented say, "Why finish high school? Why should I try? Even if I get a college degree, I can't get a job. I'll be working in poultry, running a store, or cleaning." . . . Some even thought of committing suicide.

So, what was it like after DACA? She said, "Transformational. They had hope. They had a piece of the American Dream. They would come to the office two or three hours early to learn how to apply for DACA. They knew that DACA was temporary, but they could get a Social Security number, a work permit, and a driver's license. There was no fear of deportation, and they had access to college and a real job." Mireya pointed out other benefits. "They could graduate more quickly from college. There were no public scholarships, but they could get private ones, and they could get a bank loan for school. They could help their parents, who were working two or three jobs, financially; maybe they could just work two." And, there were psychological benefits. "They came out of the shadows. Most began to try to finish high school. And they could finally talk about their status and discovered that there were many others in the same boat. It was a big relief that they could talk about it." The economic benefits were huge. "They could work in the normal economy, not the cash one. They could make more money, get a bank loan, start a new business . . . study abroad, and be better educated. It was a glimpse of what the DREAM Act would do for undocumented kids." Then she gave us the Arkansas statistics—ten thousand youth were eligible, eight thousand have benefited from the program over the years, and 5,700 were still active. We asked. "What happened to them since the September 5th announcement?" Her description was the same and as depressing as Jeanette and Laura's.

The media frames news stories by telling their audience the story but also the way it could be interpreted. Framing has been central in shaping of the immigration debate, and Mireya knows the importance of framing the AUCC message. An Arkansas DREAM Act, giving in-state tuition to undocumented youth who had graduated from a state high school, was the organization's first campaign. At first, the opponents controlled the framing and vilified parents for bringing their children to the United States. Immigrants were portrayed as law-breakers who took Americans' jobs and used Americans' social services, but without paying any taxes. At first, AUCC was reactive, then quickly became proactive.

Mireya described AUCC's frame. "First, we focused on the role our government and businesses played in creating unauthorized immigration. Trade policies like NAFTA destroyed entire economic sectors in Mexico and other countries in Latin America. Our foreign policies in Central America escalated the violence and prolonged the civil wars giving people few alternatives but to migrate." And finally, "Employers in this country exploited the unauthorized labor force because they knew the government weakly enforced our labor laws."

Mireya then shared AUCC's positive frame. AUCC showcases the educational success and vital roles that the DACAmented play in our economy. They remind us that DACAmented youths have ties to their country of origin, are bilingual and bicultural, and can navigate multiple societies with ease. But she also made an important distinction between integration (becoming part) and the melting pot (blending and disappearing). AUCC believes that there is significant economic value in holding onto one's language, culture, and ties to the country of origin. "We work in a global economy, and immigrants bring a unique set of skills to our economy and society," she says.

Mireya reflected on DACA. "DACA is gone. Protection from deportation and work permits is scheduled to begin phasing out on March 5, 2018. Any ICE or law enforcement contact can lead to deportation, so there is a sense of urgency." She reminded us, "Never bet on politics," and feels there will probably be no solution until the next Congress. She may be right. It is February 2018, and the Senate has failed to pass any legislation.[2] The Senate bills debated addressed the same issues: (1) the legal status of the undocumented, (2) a path to citizenship, (3) family reunification, and (4) annual immigration numbers. They range from a DREAM Act of 2017 that addresses only undocumented youth, to ones that include border security and a wall, to ones that curtail family reunification and dramatically reduce legal immigration. Like Laura, Mireya finds disturbing the proposals that grant lawful status but no path to citizenship and curtail family reunification. Like our other allies she feels that all people in the United States should have the same constitutional rights, and if you live here and pay taxes, you should have a path to citizenship. A law should continue the fifty-year policy of family reunification. Similarly, she feels that the Dreamers are political pawns and a divided Congress will not carry out the will of the American people. Activism, she notes, is vital in bringing the political pressure needed for reform. She sees some encouraging trends: Dreamers are speaking out. They are emerging as leaders. They have allies in our business, educational, and political leadership. And don't forget the support by many of the Fortune 500 companies who were founded by immigrants or children of immigrants.

Figure 5.4
Luis Restrepo, director of the Comparative Literature and Cultural Studies Program, with his seminar students. © 2018 University Relations.

Luis Restrepo

When he was the director of La Oficina Latino—the Office of Latino Academic Advancement and Community Relations—Luis Restrepo played a critical role in bridging the gap between the university and the state's Latino population. He reached out to students and their parents, provided a role model for the campus's Latino students, and helped create a safe and welcoming campus for all. We interviewed Dr. Restrepo in his campus office on September 29, 2017, two weeks after the Trump administration's announcement that DACA had ended.

Our first question was, "What is your role as a college professor and administrator in the DACA debate?" He paused for a moment and said, "I am a college professor teaching at a public university that should be open to everyone. If it is not open to everyone, a public university is reproducing privilege and leaving people behind." He then spoke of undocumented youth, and how they are being penalized because their parents decided to bring them here. He is still disturbed by the Arkansas Board of Higher Education's decision in 2008 to end in-state tuition for the undocumented. "They are forced to pay three times more, . . . which is punitive and means higher education is not for all."

"How has DACA affected your students? Has the policy transferred into the classroom?" Luis talked about his empathy for his students and wonders what it must be like to live in constant fear—living in a community where a traffic stop means being deported from the only country you know. He also talked about what it must be like to be living in the shadows, working illegally, and being treated like a criminal. He said, "I cannot imagine a situation like this."

But then he spoke fondly of his memories of the months following the announcement of DACA—how "his students shared their excitement with him when they got their first Social Security card or shared a text with a picture of their driver's license." He reflected on the emotional toll the last few months have had on his students. He remembers students crying out of fear before DACA, and how they cried after the September 5th announcement as they saw "all they have known coming to an end."

Luis admires his undocumented students. At first, he didn't know how to respond to Dreamers because he thought their problems were insurmountable. He saw undocumented students begin to organize and create hope. "I have watched these Dreamers; they are like the civil rights generation. They see a cause. They see injustice, and they are getting mobilized." He admires how these students have come forward, out of the shadows, unafraid, and fighting this injustice.

Luis sees the most significant impact of DACA in his class for Spanish Heritage Speakers. Students write their autobiography in the course, telling their stories of how they came here, and the lives they are living here. He shared that they have a "sense that they are not fully American. . . . That they have no rights. . . . That they live in limbo." He sees the ways—big and small—they are stymied by their undocumented status. Although many of them are excellent students, they can't get scholarships or loans. He remembers a decade ago, when students first needed a Social Security number to apply to the University of Arkansas or any other public university in the state. This change in state policy meant they "had to confront that instead of paying $20,000 a year it would be between $30 to $40,000 like international students."

This change priced most of them out of a college education. He shared an example of a student who had only five courses left to graduate, and thought she couldn't graduate. Her mother worked in the service industry and the added cost of out-of-state tuition was an insurmountable barrier. She despaired, "How could her family earn an additional $10,000?"

So, what will happen in March? Luis thinks it will be "very costly to politicians to uproot nearly one million people." He can't imagine deporting so many successful students. "They are in college, they have undergraduate degrees, and some are in graduate school." But he has hope that Congress will find a compromise because Luis has faith in our democracy and the power of elections. He has "Faith in the power of the people. Faith in the power of justice, and in the power of faith communities that have been vocal and supported undocumented students." He puts special faith in students. "Students cannot remain silent because they have a privilege and with that privilege comes a responsibility to make sure that the door stays open and that it is not shut by injustice." His solution is legislation similar to the amnesty program for the undocumented during the Reagan administration or the truth and reconciliation process after the civil wars in Africa and Central America. It is called "transitional justice." "You are not throwing justice out, but creating a framework by which you can stop the condition and the society can move forward." So, he thinks, "What we need is a transitional framework to routinize the [immigration] process, do justice to the families, and stop punishing children."

Final Thoughts

In this chapter, we have heard from a teacher, an attorney, a community activist, and a college professor who work daily with undocumented youth. I call them allies because they are committed to the causes of immigration reform and social justice. There were familiar themes in their interviews—the fear, anxiety, and the hopelessness the undocumented felt before DACA, and the hope and optimism they felt after the creation of DACA. We learned that the program was successful. The region's DACAmented are going to college, completing their degrees, pursuing graduate and professional work, and entering the workforce where they are employed by some of the nation's largest corporations. We learned that they are marrying, having children, buying homes, and becoming part of the fabric of their communities, and many are leaders in their communities. We also learned of their emotional roller coaster as they relive their undocumented past, and how the September 5th announcement foretells lost jobs and the specter of deportation. We learned of their anger and their commitment to activism and peaceful protest. But more than anything we learned of a broken political system where our leaders ignore the will of the vast majority of the Americans who want immigration reform with a path to citizenship for undocumented youth.

In the next chapter, I share the stories of two remarkable DACA recipients, Juan Mendez and Zessna Garcia Rios, whom I profiled in my 2012 book, *Right To DREAM: Immigration Reform and America's Future*. It's been seven years since I last interviewed them, and, as you will see, with DACA protections they have done remarkable things with their lives.

SIX

Old Friends

Zessna Garcia Rios and Juan Mendez

In fall 2013, I received a call from Nick Perilla, the assistant to Henry Cisneros, the former secretary of the Department of Housing and Urban Development in the Clinton administration. Nick wanted to set up a meeting with the secretary and me because Cisneros wanted to pick my brain. A cabinet member and the former mayor of San Antonio wanted to pick my brain? Turns out that he had heard about my research on the region's Hispanic community, and he was interested in launching a pilot program in Northwest Arkansas. He did and it became known as the American Dream Initiative. The initiative focused on communities that had "experienced a significant recent growth in new immigrant populations and where the infrastructure for immigrant integration was not fully developed." The program would "engage stakeholders to work with new immigrants whose economic and cultural presence merits greater understanding." And the program would—first, "improve access for new immigrants to the resources and services they need to pursue the American Dream," and second, "instill a sense of urgency about education in new immigrant families by engaging family members in educational goals and breaking down barriers to academic achievement." The principal human capital "to carry out these strategies was an American Dream Corps of talented young professionals and established community leaders." Known as American Dream Fellows, they would be chosen through a competitive national search and would work at the grassroots level in the region.[1]

Figure 6.1

Zessna Garcia Rios teaching her American National Government class.
© 2018 University Relations

Zessna Garcia Rios

Henry Cisneros introduced the program and the first class of the American Dream Fellows to Northwest Arkansas in a packed theater on the University of Arkansas's campus on October 23, 2014. A few weeks later there was a call for the second class of fellows, and I nominated Zessna Garcia Rios. On April 24, 2015, nine candidates for the fellowships were flown to San Antonio for two days of grueling interviews. The pool included recent graduates from Oxford University, Harvard, Johns Hopkins, and Zessna from the University of Arkansas. I was there, and I have never experienced an interview process as intense and exhausting. Over the next two days, each candidate met with five panels composed of former ambassadors, national leaders in the Latino movement, executives of Fortune 500 Companies, and Cisneros. A few weeks later, the Cisneros Center announced its choices, and Zessna Garcia Rios became an American Dream Fellow.

I interviewed Zessna in February 2018, and my first question focused on her interview for the fellowship. She said, it was "one of the most nerve-wracking experiences of my life. I had four or five interviews in one day with not only some of the most powerful people in Texas but also the nation." During her interviews, she spoke frankly to the panel members about why working in nonprofits that focused on immigrant communities was so close to her heart. "Until the interview, I didn't know I could get beyond my life's hurdles. After talking to Mr. Cisneros and the board, I felt that there was nothing to stop me if I had the right resources. If this is what DACA has done for me, imagine what would happen if we gave resources to the entire immigrant population." She described her work as a fellow in the region's immigrant communities and how the programs she had helped launch are now part of programs run by the corporations and nonprofits.

Arrival and Early Childhood

Zessna's story parallels the stories of many Dreamers. Her parents brought her to the United States when she was three and the family settled in Bentonville, Arkansas. Zessna's parents came for jobs and economic opportunity. Her family had a successful butcher shop in Gomez Palacio, Durango, Mexico, until her grandfather died. She recalls her parents' story, "No one was able to take care of the shop because everyone was too young. So, while this was all happening, everyone started looking for different ways to help out the family. A couple of them moved north and settled here."

As do many immigrants, Zessna's family followed a migration stream that links their hometown with their destination. Today, Zessna has twenty-five cousins and eight aunts and uncles living in Northwest Arkansas. "My parents' original plan was to be here only for a couple of years, raise enough money to pay for their home in Mexico, and go back home and continue their life there. That is the plan that everyone has. Work for a bit, send money back, and go back, but it doesn't happen for most of us because this becomes home."

Like many undocumented, Zessna lives in a mixed-status family—among her siblings, she is the only one undocumented. It was interesting to hear her talk about the integration of her siblings. Zessna speaks Spanish fluently with the lilt that comes from living in Northern Mexico. Her sister Erika's Spanish is very formal, her sister Jessica's

Figure 6.2
Zessna and her grandfather at her fifth birthday party. Permission by the Garcia Rios family.

Spanish is a little less formal, but her little brother, Jesus, speaks broken Spanish. This is a pattern across the region. Some school districts in Northwest Arkansas bring translators to parent-teacher conferences because only the children in the family speak English.

Activism

Zessna's activism began during a workshop in Conway, Arkansas in March 2010. Organized by United We Dream, the nation's largest Dreamer organization, participants learned how to tell their stories and how to craft an elevator speech. They also learned what not to say. They learned how to put events together, frame their messages, and use the media effectively. Following the workshop, Zessna started talking to students at her high school while she worked with Juan Mendez and other area Dreamers regarding next steps. In May

2010 she, Juan, and another close friend drove to Delaware to help kick start the Delaware DREAM Team. "We were there for a little less than a month, and we were able to set it all up. We left the state in good hands," reflected Zessna. Their work in Wilmington shaped their efforts in launching the Arkansas Natural Dreamers. Later in the summer at a meeting with national coordinator of United We Dream, their Arkansas organization became an affiliate.

The Run-Up to the Obama Administration's DACA Announcement and DACA

Zessna kept contact with United We Dream, and the night before the announcement, she received the text, "Get ready for an announcement tomorrow. Get together everything you have to prove your existence here." Nervousness, negativity, fear, and hope were in the air, but Zessna was optimistic. She thought if the national Dreamer organization texted that an announcement was coming, then it must be good news. She was right. She recalls, "I was stunned, relieved, and hopeful. Stunned because it was something that we would never have expected. I was relieved that I wouldn't have to live in fear. And I was hopeful in the sense that I felt that this was the first step in getting something more permanent."

When asked how DACA had changed her life, she responded:

> My life changed drastically. I went from baby-sitting and working construction and doing odd jobs to having opportunity. Never had I thought I would have a choice of what I wanted to do, have a choice in where I wanted to work. . . . It opened so many doors, and I was able to explore my wants and needs. Before the only jobs I could get had to pay cash. . . . I knew [these jobs] had to be done and I was happy to do them, but they weren't what I wanted to do the rest of my life. With DACA, I had the opportunity to change careers and roles, to work in the nonprofit and corporate sectors, and in education. It opened up my mind on the possibilities and opened up my life.

She described other DACA benefits. It helped her get her bachelor's degree faster—four years at a community college and four years at the University of Arkansas. Before DACA, she could afford only one or two classes per semester because of out-of-state tuition. With DACA, she could earn higher wages, enabling her to take three and four classes each semester. She said, "Never in my wildest dreams did I think this was going to happen; I'm going to finish."

Opportunities opened up for Zessna immediately after graduation. She spent a year as an American Dream Fellow, and then became a health educator in a program at the University of Arkansas Medical School. Funded by the National Institutes of Health, it was an initiative to provide culturally appropriate health care to the region's ethnic communities with the goal to reduce type 2 diabetes, an epidemic in these communities. But her most treasured opportunity was pursuing a graduate degree in political science at the University of Arkansas. She received a privately funded scholarship, and in spring 2018 is teaching a section of American national government to seventy freshmen and sophomores. "Never in my life did I think DACA would allow me to get a graduate degree and that I would be teaching American government!"

Zessna says that her students know she is DACAmented. On the first day of class, she introduced herself and shared her work experience. She described her lobbying work with corporate leaders on major policy issues, and in the course of her conversation, a student asked, "What was the policy issue?" She told them, "The DREAM Act." Another student asked, "What's the DREAM Act?" She outlined the DREAM Act and DACA, and then came right out, "The issue is important to me because I am DACAmented." And then she described what it was, whom it helps, and why it is important. I ask her how did her students respond? "My students don't have an issue with it. They don't doubt my credentials."

The Election

Zessna's major in college was journalism, and we talked about how the political parties framed the immigration issue in the 2016 election. She said the "Left frame" was the successful immigrant—the lawyer, the neurosurgeon, and the professional with an advanced degree who was making a contribution to the high end of our economy. The

"Right's frame" was hoodlum kids, taking American's jobs, not paying taxes, and destroying the country's economy. These stories play to the parties' bases, but like our political parties who have ignored the voters in the center, the frames leave out the stories of immigrants who live their lives in the middle. We seldom hear about what life is like for most immigrants in this society: working hard, raising children, managing relationships with family and friends, just doing the things of an ordinary life.

When I asked what her feelings were like on election night, Zessna replied that like most Americans she started the evening assuming Hillary Clinton was going to win the election. As the night wore on and states began to flip red, she realized that Trump was going to be the next president. "It was a little hurtful and downright scary. The narrative on the Right was so negative that we knew that programs like DACA were going to end and that there would be no immigration reform any time soon."

What were you thinking during the run up to the Trump administration's announcement that DACA would be rescinded? "We knew that something bad was going to happen from the campaign and statements from Trump and his cabinet." During a graduate seminar in Latino politics, Zessna stepped out into the hall to answer a phone call from a local reporter. When she returned, the class was quiet. When she looked into the faces of her classmates, she knew the worst had happened. She said, "I was upset, but I tried to be positive. I told my classmates that this is going to be one of the times in history where you will remember where you were and whom you were with." She went on to say, "This is why we need to vote. This is why we need to actively participate in our elections. What do the polls show? Eighty percent of Americans are in favor of legalization for undocumented students. We have people in office who speak for only one group in this country, and we need to broaden the conversation."

After class, she texted her friends, "How are you doing? Are you feeling okay? Is there anything I can do to help?" And a dear friend texted back, "I'm on campus and everyone around me is acting like nothing has happened, and my world has just fallen apart." Zessna sought to reassure her that this isn't the end and they will pull through.

Zessna is an optimistic person. She looks at the positive outcomes of DACA. She believes that DACA has allowed undocumented youth to build a platform for change. "We have shown the American people we can make a contribution to this society . . . we are becoming educators, lawyers, nurses, the pillars of our communities. We now have a platform that no one can take away from us. We can use it for our next steps."

Zessna will lose her protected status in two years. The day before the announcement she was at the United States Immigration and Customs Services' office in Fort Smith, Arkansas, renewing her deferment. I asked, "You have two years. What happens if we don't get immigration reform? Does it mean you are back in the shadows? Living in fear?" She answered, "Yes and no. Yes, I will be out of status; but, no, I won't be in fear. I have come out. I have lived a life like someone who has documents, who is living a normal life. I am not going to lose hope because we have proven what we can do for this country . . . if nothing resolves in those two years there is no way my spirit will ever be broken."

I asked her about the legislation pending in the Senate. Zessna believes solving the problem of the million-plus Dreamers could provide a framework for comprehensive immigration reform. As a political science student, she appreciates the competing interest groups and the complexity of the issues. She pointed to the need to reform the application process, especially for those who seek to emigrate from countries with political and economic problems. Asked about the eleven million undocumented presently living in the United States, Zessna noted that the average undocumented person has lived in the United States for more than ten years and is part of their communities. She thinks that the Obama administration's executive order, Deferred Action for Parents of Americans and Lawful Permanent Residents (DAPA) was a good first step. Although blocked in the federal courts, it would have granted deferred action to unauthorized adults who had lived in the United States since 2010 and had children who are either American citizens or lawful permanent residents. DACA and DAPA would have provided deferments for half of the undocumented. Deferred action is not full legal status, but with a multiyear renewable work permit and exemption from deportation, the programs would have gone a long way in solving the nation's undocumented problem.

My last question was: "What would you like people forty or fifty years from now to know about immigration and immigration reform now?" She reflected, "I would like them to know that our immigrant population was resilient and hopeful. We were just regular people trying to live our lives. And we had some incredible hurdles but managed to live our lives happily."

Juan Mendez

I first met Juan Mendez in 2009 at a meeting organized by former University of Arkansas chancellor G. David Gearhart. The Arkansas Department of Higher Education had introduced a policy requiring a Social Security number to be included on the state's college admissions forms. Chancellor Gearhart recognized the policy would create a $9,000 increase in tuition for undocumented students, so he assembled campus leaders to discuss how the university could help make higher education accessible and affordable to the growing number of

Figure 6.3
Juan Mendez, DACAmented, a DREAMer, and a successful businessman photographed in front of the Monarch Butterfly Migrating Mural, Springdale, Arkansas. ©2018 University Relations

undocumented students in the state. Juan attended the meeting. Out of the meeting came a number of strategies, and the idea for my 2012 book, *Right to DREAM: Immigration Reform and America's Future.* When I interviewed him for the first book, Juan was nineteen years old. He's now twenty-eight, married, and a homeowner with a career at Walmart. I interviewed Juan on February 7, 2018. His story, like Zessna's, shows what can happen when we allow undocumented youth to fully participate in our society and economy.

Arrival and Early Years

Juan was seven when his parents brought him to the United States. His family's hometown is two hours south of Presidio, Texas. His parents were married in their late teens, and as Juan describes it, "Our economic status wasn't all that bad." His dad had two years of college, but in Mexico, "You have to know somebody that knows somebody that knows somebody to be able to get into school and get a scholarship." When his father lost his contact, he had to leave school. His father first tried importing goods from the United States for resale, but he didn't make enough to support his family. He then opened a restaurant, but corruption and violence made it very difficult. "We tried every single thing in Mexico to make money, to make a living, but it just wasn't possible."

It was clear that the family didn't have much of a future in Chihuahua State, Mexico. Economic opportunity draws the vast majority of immigrants to the United States, and this is borne out in Juan's story. Juan's father illustrates another point that those who emigrate are different from those who stay behind. Moving to another society is fraught with risk, and immigrants who come here for economic opportunities tend to be better educated, more motivated, and entrepreneurial. Bottom line: it is a transfer of human capital from the sending society to the receiving society.

Juan's family arrived in Springdale, Arkansas, on September 17, 1997. They were able to cross the border on a tourist visa. As with many immigrants to the United States, they were part of an immigration stream that linked their hometown to a US city. Juan's mother had a sister who lived in Springdale.

Figure 6.4
Juan's school picture at John Tyson Elementary School, Springdale, Arkansas, 1998. Photo provided by Juan Mendez.

Juan's earliest memory of Springdale was John Tyson Elementary. He notes, "It's a wonderful school, but it was also evident that Springdale wasn't ready for the Hispanic population explosion at the time." He had a "wonderful teacher, who wasn't quite trained to handle someone who didn't speak English. There were three or four of us who didn't speak English. . . . She always put us in a group alone so we wouldn't slow everybody else down. We had ESL classes, but they were very slow paced. Very slow paced." Learning English was Juan's passion from his first day in school. I asked when he became fluent in English. "Maybe three or four months. . . . I had a thick accent at the time, but I was getting better." Today, Juan has an Arkansas accent.

Becoming a DREAMer Activist

Juan is one of the founders of the DREAM movement in Arkansas. In fall of 2009, Juan was asked by a DREAMer organizer to drive to Minnesota for a strategy and training meeting. It was one of the first in the nation, and the forty Dreamers who attended shaped the movement. The tag line on the state's license plate at the time was "The Natural State," so the movement became known as the Arkansas Natural Dreamers.

Juan returned to Arkansas committed and energized, and the first item on his agenda was a DREAM event at the University of Arkansas in February 2010. The local Dreamers planned to hold a rally, take its success back to the community, start working together, and hold more events that spring. Unfortunately, the weather was terrible. Rather than the three hundred demonstrators they expected, only a few dozen showed up for the rally. Most of the organizers were crestfallen, but Juan saw it differently. He said, "No, this is awesome because we are taking the step that no one has taken before." Within a year, Arkansas Natural Dreamers became an affiliate of United We Dream, the movement's national umbrella organization.

They now had a strategy. They would confront the establishment and get out their narrative. They would lobby elected officials to let them know who the Dreamers were. He remembers confronting politicians such as Blanche Lincoln and Mark Pryor—senators from Arkansas at the time—at town meetings and "pretty much wherever they showed up." "I wanted them to know my name was Juan. I wanted them to know the names of my friends and understand their struggles. I wanted them to know all we have accomplished even though we were undocumented." Good things started to happen as the support from leaders in the state's education, business, and political leadership increased. Arkansas Natural Dreamers lobbied in Washington for the DREAM Act in 2010 and, although it failed, they were part of the movement that led to the Obama administration's announcement of "deferred action."

Juan's Life Changes with DACA

Juan received a call around 3:30 AM. At the other end was a friend in Washington who told him to "wait for an announcement in the morning. We finally did it." Juan didn't know what the news was going to be, but he knew it had to be good. That morning he stayed home from work, talked to his fiancée, parents, and friends, and waited for the news. When he learned about DACA, he was at first ecstatic, but then thought of all the people who would be left out because of the age cap—his parents and all the unauthorized people who work hard, live by the rules, and deserve to live here without fear.

As it had for Zessna, the announcement transformed Juan's life. He applied for DACA and within four or five months was approved.

A few weeks later he had a driver's license. Juan said a driver's license was just a piece of plastic, but it took "a huge burden off his shoulders. Just knowing that if a police officer pulls me over, I'm not going to jail." Within a few months he bought his first car, and in another six months he bought another one. With a work permit, he secured a job with Tyson Foods. (He now works for Walmart.) With a steady income, he bought land on the edge of Springdale and on Thanksgiving Day, 2016, he and his wife moved into their new home. They built it themselves with cash and don't have a mortgage. Without DACA, they wouldn't be married and wouldn't be homeowners.

Run-Up to the 2016 Election and the September 5th Announcement

Juan was taken aback by Trump's rhetoric on immigrants. "I thought Trump would look at immigration as a businessman. Immigration is good for the economy. He hired them to work in his hotels, restaurants, and businesses. He knows how hard it is to find good workers. I thought if anyone would know how much immigrants contribute to our economy, he would."

Given the campaign rhetoric and Trump's first executive orders, Juan knew the DACA was going to end. He was emotional the day of the rescission. He said, "Just look at what we have accomplished with just a crack in the door. The rug was pulled out from under us. I was angry that we were in limbo again and back to square one." He described the psychological toll the previous months had taken on him. The first thing in the morning and the last thing at night, Juan would Google "DACA" to read about changes in the policy. The DACAmented just wanted to know what was happening so they could plan the next steps in their lives.

Previously, I described the atmosphere the evening of the rescission of DACA at the Arkansas United Community Coalition. Juan was there and tried to describe his feelings that evening. "Words are hard to come by when people's lives are turned upside down. I was seeing people with children, people coming from work, people coming from school, coming to the meeting to hear about the end of DACA. We were all in shock. . . . I was listening to what they had to say and feeling their despair and I tried to give them hope." He also talked to a few young Dreamers, and they asked him what he thought was going to happen. What should they do? He told them, "We will fight back. We will organize and create our own narrative and not allow them [Trump administration] to create one for us. We have to create awareness. We have to make our employers and schools aware of the change. We won't stay quiet."

Juan talked about changes in his hometown of Springdale following the announcement. Some anti-immigrant people felt empowered, and some of them would drive down the main streets in their pickups with their Confederate flags. But more often, he experienced the good side of the community. "People went out of their way to be supportive. Local businesses went out of their way to make me feel welcome. They realize that we are a community and that everyone who lives here contributes to the success of our businesses." He was especially pleased that the mayors of Springdale and Fayetteville wrote the president and asked him not to end DACA. And he had special praise for Springdale mayor, Doug Sprouse, who let the Dreamers know they were part of his community. But fear soon returned. The undocumented worried that ICE would expand enforcement in Springdale. Things got worse because of the mixed messages. The White House told them that they were only going after felons and gang members, but ICE had a different message—if you are here illegally, you need to be always looking over your shoulder. Juan feels that the DACA announcement destabilized his community. "Rumors spread like wildfire. We worry that there will be an uptick in ICE enforcement, and people are staying home." He is especially concerned about the DACAmented. Juan reminded us that, "The government knows where we work and where we live. There is no place to hide. There is no living in the shadows anymore. We are living totally exposed and the emotional toll is crushing."

A federal district court judge has stayed Trump's executive order, but unless Congress acts, Juan will lose his DACA protections on April 23, 2019. His wife's deferment times out this fall. They talk about their future. They have delayed having children because they don't want to chance being separated from their child. They saved and paid cash for their land and the home they built because they are safer without a mortgage. They knew that DACA was not permanent, but the day Juan loses DACA, he loses his job at Walmart and his family's financial future. "We may not have a mortgage, but we still have bills to pay." There will be an impact across the region because the DACAmented are in our workforce, and they won't have paychecks to spend in the local economy.

His future? Juan sees the psychological toll the last few months have taken on him, his family, and community. He pointed out, "You may not have noticed, but I have been clawing at the arms of this chair during the interview because I get so anxious when I talk about it. I have anxiety for my wife, and I have anxiety for my younger sister and her husband. If DACA ends, it is the end of their lives, the end of their jobs, and an end to their contributions to our economy and community." Juan notes that the DACAmented have lives here that are being taken away from them. They had huge aspirations. They had a plan for all of it. They had a future; now they live week-to-week. And if the unthinkable happens, and he loses DACA? He will no longer be working, and he will be back in the informal economy. He will miss his Walmart family and all that they have accomplished for the company.

So, what if the DREAM Act of 2018 passes? Juan said, "I could go back to sleeping at night. I would stop the constant twitching. I would have psychological tranquility, not fearing being uprooted from where I call home and being sent to a place I don't know. I would feel that my parents had accomplished what they always wanted for me. Security in this country. A better life than the one we had in Mexico. I could look at my wife and not see her worry. I hope that this country will do the right thing."

Final Thoughts

I have known Zessna and Juan for a decade. I have admired their activism, willingness to come out and live unafraid, and work to change our nation's immigration policies. But what I have learned in my research is that the themes we hear in Zessna and Juan's stories are shared by other Dreamers and the DACAmented. Their parents came to the United States for the economic opportunity, and they were better educated and better skilled than the people who stayed behind. They chose their destination to be near family. Their parents brought them here at a young age, and they lived in our neighborhoods, attended our schools, and overcame the challenges necessary to become a member of our society. They have few memories of their lives in their birth country, and they think of themselves as Americans. They lived in the shadows supporting themselves and their families in the informal cash economy. They were one-traffic stop or an ICE sweep away from deportation. Fear was always just below the surface of their consciousness. They worked tirelessly for the DREAM Act but were undeterred when it failed to pass, and their work led to the Obama administration's policy of Deferred Action for Childhood Arrivals. They met with joy the DACA announcement in 2012, but were also saddened that millions of undocumented would be left out of the policy. DACA transformed their lives. They came out of the shadows, lived without fear, and were successful. They were disturbed with the rhetoric during the 2016 campaign, shocked by Trump's election, and stoic with his administration's announcement ending DACA on September 5, 2017. They well remember their feelings that day—their anger but also their determination to fight on. A federal district court judge has stayed the executive order and given them a reprieve, but they are realists. Without a law, all they have accomplished can end in the appellate process, and their careers and their lives here would abruptly come to an end. The uncertainty this past year has taken a psychological toll. Zessna and Juan demonstrate what a DREAM Act could accomplish. In the final chapter, we explore where we have been as a society, how past generations have dealt with the immigration issue, how demographic change and the power of social movements will change our society, and the next steps that we all can and should take.

SEVEN

Next Steps

Where We Go from Here

My surname is Schwab. My paternal grandmother was a Gressle. My mother's family name was Romberger, and her mother was a Schaich. This fall, my son is marrying Maria Platzbecker, a third-generation Bavarian. Our families have been here since the early 1800s, and there is German ancestry down both sides of the family.[1] And we are not alone. More Americans trace their ancestry to Germany than any other country. (I bet you thought it was England.) So, what's not to like about Germans? Just ask our founding fathers.

Benjamin Franklin hated the Germans. In a letter to Peter Collinson in 1753, Franklin shared his concerns. He believed they were not smart. "Those who come hither are generally of the most ignorant stupid sort of their own nation." He believed they didn't embrace American values. "Not being used to liberty, they know not how to make a modest use of it." He believed they would change what it meant to be an American. "Why should Pennsylvania, founded by the English, become a Colony of Aliens, who will shortly be so numerous as to Germanize us instead of our anglicizing them, and will never adopt our language or customs, any more than they can acquire our complexion."[2]

Alexander Hamilton, himself an immigrant, viewed German immigrants with suspicion as well. He argued, "The influx of foreigners must, therefore, tend to produce a heterogeneous compound; to change and corrupt the national spirit; to complicate and confound public opinion; to introduce foreign propensities."[3] And, although Thomas Jefferson favored immigration, he wasn't too keen on the Germans, whom he thought would never assimilate. He wrote, "As in our German settlements, they preserve for a long time their own languages, habits, and principles of government."[4]

Does this sound familiar? It should, because the same themes played out in the 2016 presidential election. And, today, as in our past, it is an issue that polarizes and divides us, and for good reason: immigration is the process that shapes who we are as a people and molds our national character. We read this theme in the words of our founders, and we see it in the immigration laws passed since our founding. Each law regulated who could immigrate and who was excluded, and most of them were grounded in racism. Here are a few examples. The Naturalization Act of 1790, our first immigration law, made clear that an applicant had to be a "free white person," thus excluding Native Americans and slaves. The Chinese Exclusion Act of 1882 was our first law to exclude a specific ethnic group, and it banned Chinese laborers from immigrating for the next ten years and authorized deportation of unauthorized Chinese immigrants. The Emergency Quota Act of 1921 was the first law to create numerical quotas for immigration based on nationality. Quotas were equal to 3 percent of the foreign-born group's representation in the 1910 census. Immigration from Asian countries continued to be barred, but there were no quotas for countries in the Western Hemisphere. Similarly, the Immigration Act of 1924 tweaked the 1921 law to favor migration from Northern and Western Europe, to limit migration from Eastern and Southern Europe, to continue to bar immigration from Asian countries, and to deny entry to anyone ineligible to become a citizen due to race. Our current immigration policies are based on the Immigration and Nationality Act of 1965, which replaced the national origins quota system with a preference system emphasizing family reunification and skilled immigrants.[5] Since 1965, our immigration laws and court rulings have dealt with the control of undocumented immigration, citizenship, border security, and immigration ceilings. Given that most of our immigrants are from Latin America and Asia, these laws still have a racial undertone.

I published *Right to DREAM: Immigration Reform and America's Future* in 2012. Then, as now, misrepresentation and lies about immigrants were rampant, and I wanted to answer the critics of immigration reform. Social scientists have been studying immigration since the late nineteenth century, so it seemed important to summarize this research on central topics in the debate. Beginning each chapter, I summarized the positions of the critics on the legal, immigration, economic, cultural, and assimilation issues of the day. For example, chapter 1, "These Children Are Blameless," explores the legal issues surrounding the education of immigrant children. At the top of the first page, I stated the position of the critics, "Undocumented students are criminals. They broke the law. Passing the DREAM Act would reward criminals by extending higher education to undocumented students. The criminals should go home, get in line, and apply to enter the country legally." And I organized my response around the Supreme Court's 1982 *Plyler v. Doe* ruling because the issues settled in this case were as relevant in 2012 as they were in 1982. Undocumented children were blameless for the violation of immigration law by their parents; education is a prerequisite for full participation in our society; and it is in our national interest, our common good, that all children, regardless of immigration status, be provided public education. I still believe the DREAM Act is a straightforward extension of the *Plyler* principles to the college education of undocumented youth.

In the chapters that followed, I explored other issues central to the debate. Chapter 2, "Immigration 101," looks at the social science research on immigration. When immigrants come to the United States for jobs and economic opportunities, they are different from those who stay behind—they tend to be better educated, more highly skilled and ambitious, and they pass these qualities onto their children. Important to us, the sending society pays for the development of this human capital, and our economy benefits from this transfer of their national wealth.

Anti-immigrant groups argue that immigrants are a tax burden, don't pay for the services they use, contribute to state budget shortfalls, and take jobs from American workers. In my chapter, "Spend a $Trillion a Year and You're a Tax Burden?" I report a very different reality. Immigrants grow the economy, create jobs, pay taxes at the federal, state, and local levels, make contributions to Social Security and Medicare, and contribute more in taxes than they cost in social services. The numbers have changed in the past six years. In 2013, I reported that immigrants contributed $1.6 trillion a year to the US economy. By 2017, immigrants contributed $3 trillion to the US economy.

The nation is in the midst of the Fourth Wave of Immigration, and critics believe that the newest wave is overwhelming American culture. Really? In the chapter, "Salsa—America's #1 Condiment," I described how we have created a pluralistic society by selectively absorbing the culture from each immigrant wave. I argue that this is a process that has enriched, not diminished, American culture. There's another benefit. Our ethnic diversity has created a society tailor-made for the global economy.

In "The Melting Pot Mixed with a Few New Ingredients" chapter, I explored the process of becoming an American. The newest wave is learning English and assimilating more quickly than previous ones. Even more important, most Americans think immigration is good for this country, and an even larger number support the DREAM Act.

I rounded out the book by profiling Juan and Zessna, analyzing the DREAM Act, and suggesting next steps.

This book builds on *Right to DREAM*. I, as were the majority of Americans, was stunned by the election of Donald J. Trump, and, as a sociologist, I tried to find out why it happened. In the first chapter of this book, I describe the significant social changes that had been at work in our society for two generations and how they converged in the 2016 election. For decades, social scientists have studied the disturbing rise in the nation's inequality and the forces responsible—globalization, outsourcing, automation, and rent seeking—manipulating the economic and political system to increase one's wealth without creating new wealth. Social scientists have dutifully reported their findings in academic journals, and many have authored books, news stories, and feature articles for the general reader as well. The message was and remains clear—this society has not seen this level of inequality since the Gilded Age, and we ignore this trend at our peril. Then, as now, millions suffered, and today fifty million Americans have been left behind. The second revolution underway in American society is the Fourth Wave of Immigration that reinforces these feelings of marginalization among those who feel left behind. Today, one-in-every-four people living in the United States is a first- or second-generation immigrant. We have not seen numbers like these in a century. The growth in this figure, especially the eleven million undocumented ones, when combined with the realization that within a generation the majority of us will be from minorities—black, Asian American, and Hispanic—has furthered this resentment. Finally, I portrayed the loss of faith in the American Dream, and the growing belief that we have a rigged system that benefits the few and excludes millions of Americans. I believe growing inequality, demographic change, and loss of hope underpinned the 2016 election that brought Trump to the presidency.

In the second chapter, I shed light on the facts about immigration by using government data and reports from nonpartisan research organizations like the Migration Policy Institute and the Pew Research Center. We explored topics that ranged from the facts about our nation's immigration history of which few people are aware, to the size and characteristics of our current wave of immigrants, to DACA, to public opinion on DACA and immigration. My goal is to show that immigration is in this nation's DNA and that it plays a critical role in our renewal.

To understand DACA, the DREAM Act, and Congress's current debate on immigration reform, one needs to know where we have been. Chapter 3 described the rescission of DACA on September 5, 2017, explored a short history of the changes in our immigration laws since this nation's founding, provides details on the DREAM Act, examined the Obama administration's response to congressional gridlock by creating DACA through an executive order, and stated my concerns that the next administration could rescind his executive order. It has. Deconstructing Attorney General Jeff Sessions' announcement, we find many of his sweeping generalizations about the nation's immigration were untrue. I concluded that this policy change was ill advised. Ending DACA is forcing young immigrants back into the shadows and thrusting them into the informal labor market. I show that DACA has been an unqualified success and has benefited not only the DACA recipients but also our nation and its economy.

I opened chapter 4 with the words of Jazmin and her joy on learning of President Obama's July 15, 2012, bombshell announcement of Deferred Action for Childhood Arrivals. This chapter explored the economic, political, and social impact of this program through a series of questions such as, how many were eligible for DACA and how many received relief? Who are they? Where do they live? What are they doing? How are they doing? Are they integrating into the fabric of our communities and society? What are the costs of ending the program? How many young people face deportation? I end the chapter with the words of former Mexican president Vicente Fox who would love for DACAmented youth to return so Mexico could use the human capital the United States paid to develop.

The fight for a just and inclusive immigration system cannot happen without advocates and allies of the DACAmented. In chapter 5, I highlighted the contributions of four of them who are quietly working in the background, investing their time, money, and careers in bringing about social change.

Finally, we revisited the two undocumented youth whom I profiled in my earlier book, Juan Mendez and Zessna Garcia Rios. They put a face to the hundreds of thousands of other DACAmented youth. Through their eyes, we see how DACA transformed their lives and allowed them to contribute to their communities, our society, and the economy.

I hope this book has been informative, that you know more about the social and economic forces that are shaping this nation, and the role immigration has played in this nation's exceptional history. No nation in history has brought together more people of different races, ethnicities, and religions than the United States. And we live together in peace. It is a remarkable accomplishment and that is why we have been and, I believe, will continue to be a model for integration in our global community. But we are in perilous times.

The Trump Administration's Impact on Immigration Policy

Donald Trump, long a critic of former president Obama's use of executive orders, has used an unprecedented number of them to abolish the immigration policies of the previous administration. One week after taking office, President Trump signed an executive order suspending the entry of nationals from seven predominantly Muslim countries and suspending the nation's refugee resettlement program. The courts blocked the order, but administration lawyers quickly narrowed the scope of the original one. In a flurry of new rules, the administration directed the Department of Homeland Security to begin construction of a border wall, to construct additional detention centers, or lease space near the U.S.-Mexico border, to hire five thousand additional border patrol agents, and to instruct border patrol officers and immigration judges to send detained people to the centers pending the outcome of removal procedures. President Trump also called upon state and local governments to enter into agreements with ICE to execute federal laws by investigating, apprehending, or detaining noncitizens in their communities. Other executive orders enhanced interior enforcement by significantly broadening the categories of noncitizens who face removal, withholding federal money from sanctuary cities, ordering the hiring of ten thousand additional ICE officers, and toughening the renewal of H-1B visas for highly educated, highly skilled foreign workers.[6] In the months that followed, additional orders further reshaped this nation's immigration policies and enforcement priorities including the September 5, 2017, executive order that rescinded DACA.[7]

What are the consequences of these policy changes? First, the number of apprehensions at the U.S.-Mexico border dropped 61 percent in the first one hundred days of the Trump presidency. Trump took credit for the decline, but it was a continuation of a fifteen-year trend that saw a dramatic reduction in the number of unauthorized border crossings.[8]

Second, arrests and removal of noncitizens in the interior rose 32.6 percent, and the arrests of those without criminal records more than doubled in the first one hundred days of the Trump administration.[9]

Third, H-1B is a visa program used to attract high-skilled foreigners to work here. It's a program important to the technology sector, with many talented foreign workers vying for one of the program's eighty-five thousand visas each year. United States Citizenship and Immigrations Services has instructed its officers to review requests for renewal as thoroughly as they would initial visa applications—the action that slows down the process considerably.

Fourth, ICE agents have been directed to arrest unauthorized immigrants in courthouses and other public offices and to increase the number and frequency of sweeps.

Fifth, the flow of international students entering US colleges and universities has declined between 3 and 7 percent since Trump's election. International education professionals believe Trump's harsh anti-immigrant rhetoric along with his administration's efforts to ban travelers from majority-Muslim countries and heightened scrutiny of all foreign visitors are deterring international students. Although the US higher education sector remains the global leader in international education, many educators worry that this trend may affect this major revenue source for many of the nation's college and universities.[10]

Sixth, the headline in the British daily, *The Independent,* read "One Million Fewer British Visitors to the US Predicted as Prospective Tourists React to Trump's Victory."[11] And there is a growing concern among America's hotel chains and airlines that Donald Trump's rhetoric may have caused a slump in international travel to the United States. A travel data firm found that the average daily searches for flights to the United States have declined in ninety-nine countries since the Muslim-majority travel ban—the only major exception was Russia with a 45 percent increase in search volume for US flights.[12]

Seventh, although Trump is only in the second year of his presidency, he has had a major impact on the nation's global standing. Trump and many of his policies are broadly unpopular around the globe, and our nation's favorability ratings have declined as a result. According to a Pew Research Center survey of thirty-seven nations, only 22 percent of the public had confidence in Trump's ability to conduct international affairs. This is in sharp contrast to former president Obama who enjoyed a 64 percent approval rating. This decline is most pronounced among some of America's closest allies in Europe and Asia as well as Canada and Mexico. Perhaps more distressing is the fact that the president's disapproval ratings have affected the nation's global standing. In all regions around the world, the share of the publics with a positive view of the United States has plummeted globally since his election. Should we be concerned? Yes. Our standing affects our projection of soft power and our global diplomatic efforts [13]

Eighth, Trump's immigration policies do not reflect the will of the American people. Gallup and other mainstream polls show that Americans view immigration positively.[14] More important, the overwhelming majority of Americans, regardless of political party, support the Dream Act, including a path to citizenship for undocumented youth.[15]

Finally, is this the society we want to be? I know from the national polling data that the answer is a resounding "no." So, what can we do?

The Long View: Patience—Let Generational and Demographic Change Work

Social change is any change in our social relationships and social structure. It happens all the time. Some change is dramatic like the changes that took place after 9/11, but most social change is gradual, so slow that you barely notice it but becomes significant over time. Some change is intentional, but most of the time it is unplanned. Some change is controversial such as our current debates on immigration, sexual harassment, and guns, and these debates can lead to social movements that transform our laws and society. And some changes matter more than others—changes in tastes and fashion are of little significance but changes in norms, values, and beliefs transform our society. There are two types of social change important to understanding the trajectory of immigration reform—intragenerational and intergenerational social change.[16]

Intragenerational social change refers to the change in the attitudes, beliefs, and behaviors within a generation. The change can be rapid, often short-lived, and frequently tied to a stage in the life cycle like the teen years. For example, each generation has its own fads, crazes, fashions, slang, and icons. Often whimsical, ephemeral, and fleeting, they can be gone in months or a few years. Companies such as The Gap, which tie their fortunes to the tastes of teens, face an existential crisis. But new values and beliefs that emerge in a generation can have a transformational effect on society over time because throughout our history, no generation has ever been the same as the one born before it.

This leads to the second type of social change, intergenerational. Intergenerational change occurs more slowly but results in a basic change in a society's character. It occurs as the older generation dies off, and is replaced by a younger one with different beliefs and values. As an example, consider same-sex marriage. The data in table 7.1 make the point. In May 2017, Gallup reported that support for gay marriage edged to a new high, 64 percent. For the first time, a majority of Protestants supported gay marriage, and 72 percent of Americans supported same-sex relationships.[17] But that's only part of the story—the devil is in the details. Table 7.1 also provides a glimpse in the change

Table 7.1 Support for Legal Same-Sex Marriage by Age, 1996, 2010, and 2013

Age	Percentage who say it should be legal, 1996	Percentage who say it should be legal, 2010	Percentage who say it should be legal, 2013	Change, 1996–2013 (percentage points)
18 to 29 years	41	52	70	+29
30 to 49 years	30	53	53	+23
50 to 64 years	15	40	46	+31
65 + years	14	28	41	+27

Source: McCarthy, Justin. 2015. "Record-High 60% of Americans Support Same-Sex Marriage." http://news.gallup.com/poll/183272/record-high-americans-support-sex marriage.aspx, accessed Mar 5, 2018.

of support for legal same-sex marriage by age groups. First, note that there has been a profound change in attitudes on gay marriage across age groups since 1996, but also note that the most liberal views are among the eighteen to twenty-nine year olds: 70 percent support it. Attitudes become more conservative with each subsequent older generation—only 41 percent of those sixty-five years and older support it.[18] Here's the point: as time passes and the older generation dies off, a younger generation with more liberal views replaces it, making lasting change in the nation's beliefs about interpersonal relationships. As George Will once remarked about Millennials, "To this generation, being gay is like being left-handed."[19] And the importance of intergenerational change to the immigration debate is that we are in the midst of two profound population changes—generational and demographic. Millennials are the children of the Boomers and these two generations are the nation's largest generations. The Pew Research Center has been studying Millennials for more than a decade. Turning thirty-seven this year, the oldest Millennials are well into adulthood, and the youngest are in their early twenties. This is what Pew had to say about them.

> Millennials are on the cusp of surpassing Baby Boomers as the nation's largest living adult generation, according to population projections from the US Census Bureau. As of July 1, 2016 (the latest date for which population estimates are available), Millennials, whom we define as ages twenty to thirty-five in 2016, numbered seventy-one million, and Boomers (ages fifty-two to seventy) numbered seventy-four million. Millennials are expected to overtake Boomers in population in 2019 as their numbers swell to seventy-three million, and Boomers decline to seventy-two million. Generation X (ages thirty-six to fifty-one in 2016) is projected to pass the Boomers in population by 2028.[20]

The reign of the Baby Boomers is diminishing, and as the Boomer generation ages and dies, they are being replaced by Generation Xers and Millennials who have more liberal views on immigration. Millennials will soon be the largest generation and the largest voting bloc. As the Boomers before them, they will not only shape this nation's tastes, but also its policies and beliefs about the inclusion and integration of immigrants. Let's compare the two generations.

A generation is a group whose length spans the years from birth to adulthood. They share a common age location in history, attitudes and behavior traits, and collective identity. The Boomers were born between 1946 and 1964, and this generation produced idealists and individualists. It was a generation that helped to break down barriers on sexual expression, race relationships, and the role of women in our society. However, it was a generation bedeviled with negative youth trends like drug use and teen pregnancy. This generation now holds the nation's economic and political power.

Millennials, from their first birth year in 1981 to their last year in 1996, are a generation of positive youth trends. Whether it be the low rates of homicides, violence, suicides, teen pregnancy, or good measures of child well-being, Millennials score better than previous generations. Important to immigration policy, Millennials are the most racially and ethnically diverse generation in American history, most likely to be second-generation immigrants. Many have been raised in diverse communities and schools, and they are known for their inclusiveness. Each generation breaks with the previous generation's pop culture. They correct the mistakes of their parents and leaders, and they fill the social roles vacated by the older, dying generation. Millennials will soon have their turn. Trump will probably be the last Baby Boomer president and with his passing will come younger leaders who will change our immigration policies.

Demographic change is the other potent force that will change our society and its policies. If you commit to memory just one statistic on immigration, it should be that today more than forty-three million immigrants live in our midst. When you add to this number the children with at least one foreign-born parent, you see that 25 percent of our population is either a first- or second-generation immigrant. The demographic die is cast. We can seal our borders, but in a generation, there will not be a majority of any racial or ethnic group in this nation—we will be a minority-majority society. And although Trump was elected, in part, because of the low turnout of Hispanic and black voters, Trump's anti-immigrant rhetoric and his administration's policies will probably change the course of the midterm elections. The recent wins by Democrats in Virginia, Alabama, and Pennsylvania may be a prelude to the outcome of elections in November 2018 and beyond.

The Short View: Social Movements and Next Steps

A social movement is an organized group who works to promote or resist change through collective action. In this democracy—where the free exchange of ideas is protected by the First Amendment, policy outcomes are not predetermined, ideas are freely debated in the public realm, and a free press plays a vital role in protecting our democracy—social movements are common and have played a pivotal role throughout this nation's history. In my lifetime, the civil rights, feminist, gay rights, anti-war, and environmental movements have changed us in fundamental ways. They have allowed marginalized groups to participate more fully in our society, ended the Vietnam War, and protected our environment.

Social movements continue to shape us, but with the advent of social media, they operate on steroids. Look at the fall from grace of

Harvey Weinstein, the Hollywood movie mogul. On October 5, 2017, *The New York Times* published an article reporting that at least eight women had made legal settlements with Weinstein over his sexual harassment. Since that revelation, the Weinstein Company has ousted him from his own company. He has subsequently been arrested and charged with rape, criminal sex acts, sex abuse, and sexual misconduct for alleged incidents involving two separate women. His company is being sold and a lawsuit was filed demanding the proceeds from the sale go to his victims. Weinstein is a pariah, his wife and children have left him, his bankruptcy is looming, and the #MeToo movement appeared overnight. #MeToo quickly identified the indefensible behavior of other men. The Senate ousted Al Franken, NBC fired Matt Lauer, and the list of politicians and business leaders forced out by their reprehensible behavior grows by the day. Recently, the #MeToo movement contributed to the resignation of the entire board from USA Gymnastics amid a sexual abuse scandal, and every sector of our society is under scrutiny. Women have been empowered to come forward, share their experiences, and seek justice. And they have allies—husbands, fathers, brothers, friends, coworkers, parishioners, and politicians. In months, there has been a redefinition of what is appropriate behavior in our workplaces and personal lives, and the movement has changed our society forever.

For this reason, sociology has been interested in social movements for most of its history, and it has developed theories to explain them. The "Value-Added Theory," one of the more important ones, describes how grievances turn into generalized beliefs and then into social movements. The theory maintains that social movements follow a predictable lifecycle: structural conduciveness, structural strain, generalized beliefs, precipitating factors, mobilization for action, and social control. Let's apply it to the #MeToo Movement. *Structural Conduciveness*—our democracy's history of social movements that encourages collective action. *Structural Change*—the growing participation of women in the workforce. *Growth and Spread of a Generalized Belief*—a growing number of women who have been harassed, who believe that the rules of the workplace encourage men, who feel that they have no recourse when abused, and who have thought about solutions to the problem. *Participating Factor*—an act that confirms the generalized belief, e.g., the Weinstein revelations. *Mobilization for Action*—the meteoritic rise of #MeToo reassures members that their actions address their grievances. *Social Control*—pushback from the establishment, e.g., Trump's call for due process to protect men unjustly accused of harassment and changes in the law that protect women in the workplace.

I described in detail the rise of the DREAM movement in my book, *Right to DREAM: Immigration and America's Future*. I find the movement remarkable for many reasons—its grassroots origins, its emerging leadership, its help from civil rights leaders, its adoption of the strategy of nonviolence, its mobilization of undocumented youth, allies, and money, its savvy retail politics, and its bare-knuckled threats against President Obama in the run-up to the 2012 campaign. They couldn't get a DREAM Act, but they did get an executive order creating Deferred Action for Childhood Arrivals. All the more remarkable, the movement was crafted by people who were not citizens; but young people who came out of the shadows, stood up undocumented and unafraid, and put themselves in peril for deportation by speaking publicly, demonstrating, participating in sit-ins in immigration and customs headquarters, politicians' offices, detention centers, and courthouses. It's time to finish the campaign that they began a generation ago, and the ingredients are in place. Let's take a look at the Value-Added Approach. *Structural Conduciveness*—social movements are ingrained in our political culture. *Structural Strain*—one-out-of-four Americans is a first or second- generation immigrant, eleven million undocumented people live within our midst, and there are a million undocumented youth at risk. *Growth and Spread of a Generalized Belief*—large majorities of voters in both parties support a DREAM Act, including a path to citizenship. *Precipitating Factor*—who would think the mass murder of seventeen high school students at Marjory Stoneman Douglas High School in Parkland, Florida on February 14, 2018 would change the debate on gun control after decades of carnage in our schools, movie theaters, music venues, and military bases. Why now? That's the funny thing about social movements. Like an earthquake, you know it's coming, but not when. It hasn't happened yet, but there will be an event—a bloody ICE raid, the children of an undocumented mother dragged into a deportation center, a neo-Nazi or white supremacist group's attack on peaceful demonstrators, or an outrageous statement by a politician.

It hasn't happened, but I believe it is coming. And then there will be *Mobilization for Action*. Like Mireya Reith and the Arkansas United Community Coalition, there are people and groups with plans in place and, and then, of course, there will be a response, *Social Control Factors*—immigration laws passed and a predictable backlash from anti-immigrant groups.

Remember the words to the Pledge of Allegiance. "I pledge allegiance to the flag of the United States of America, and to the republic for which it stands, one nation under God, indivisible, with liberty and justice for all." Our founders did not imbue our society's power to a king, or an aristocracy or a church, or an elected official, but to the people. We do not owe our ultimate loyalty to a president but to a constitution. As citizens, we must participate in our political process and contribute to the change that renews our nation. This book has been an exploration of the forces that brought us to this stage in our history—the profound social and economic forces that converged to bring President Trump to the White House; the massive wave of immigration that will create a society that has no majority; and a reminder that immigration is such a divisive issue because it is the process that defines our national character. Ours is one of a handful of nations in the world that was created by immigrants and through this process, our nation in many ways has become the envy of the world.

We are at that place again; once again we have millions of strangers in our midst, and once again we will live through the process that will make them Americans. You only need to look to our past to see our future. In a few generations, we will not have Mexican-Americans or Chinese-Americans or Jordanian-Americans because the hyphen will disappear and these groups will just be Americans. They will likely only speak English, only eat their special meals on holidays, marry someone outside their group, and their identity will not be with their country of origin but here. That's the American way.

For the past year, our immigration politics have focused on the plight of eight hundred thousand young people who were brought here illegally by their parents, raised in our schools and communities, and became adults pursuing higher education, working, raising families, and becoming part of the fabric of our communities; they have embraced the American Dream. And if we have the political will to solve the problem of the Dreamers, we will have made the first step in resolving our larger immigration issues. It is important that we act because immigration reform is inextricably tied to our future. If you are as disturbed as I about the pain and uncertainty we have inflicted on these young people, it is time to become involved. Simply heed the words of Laura Ferner, the immigration attorney in Springdale, Arkansas, "Get the word out. Get more people to know about the problem. Care about the cause. Get involved and understand the process. And if you have the passion, invest your time and money."

NOTES

1. THE RISE OF TRUMP AND A CLIMATE OF FEAR

1. Cillizz, Chris. 2016. "The 13 Most Amazing Findings in the 2016 Exit Poll," *Washington Post*, https://www.washingtonpost.com/news/the-fix/wp/2016/11/10/the-13-most-amazing-things-in-the-2016-exit-poll/?utm_term=.8600f60172ed, accessed May 29, 2018; and Tyson, Alec and Shiva Maniam. 2016. "Behind Trump's Victory: Divisions by Race, Gender, Education," Pew Research, http://www.pewresearch.org/fact-tank/2016/11/09/behind-trumps-victory-divisions-by-race-gender-education/, accessed May 29, 2018.

2. In reading this section, you may think that I'm an economic determinist; I'm far from it. Yes, the major reasons for the growing inequality in our society are globalization and the rise of information- and knowledge-based economy, but there are also other potent forces at work as well. There are the rent-seeking strategies by the wealthy to get more out of the economy than they contribute, the ability of the wealthy to influence economic and taxation policies, disinvestment in the education and skills of the workforce, and the rise of a plutocracy to mention a few.

3. I have based this section on chapter 2, "Globalization and Urbanization in the More-Developed World" in my book, *Deciphering the City* (Upper Saddle River, NJ: Prentice Hall, 2005). My discussion was framed by Thomas Friedman's 1999 book, *The Lexus and the Olive Tree: Understanding Globalization* 2000, and his other works on the impact of globalization on societies in the more and less developed world.

4. Robert Reich, the secretary of labor during the Clinton administration, in a series of books published over the past twenty-five years, has described changes in the global economy and their impact on the American economy and workforce. In this section, I have drawn on his 1991 work, *The Work of Nations: Preparing Ourselves for the 21st Century Capitalism* 1991. He carries this book's themes through most of his other works.

5. Moretti, Enrico. 2012. *The New Geography of Jobs*. (New York: Houghton Mifflin Harcourt, 2012).

6. Kochhar, Rakesh and Anthony Cilluffo. 2017. "How Wealth Inequality Has Changed in the US since the Great Recession, by Race, Ethnicity and Income," Urban Institute, http://www.pewresearch.org/fact-tank/2017/11/01/how-wealth-inequality-has-changed-in-the-u-s-since-the-great-recession-by-race-ethnicity-and-income/, accessed November 10, 2017.

7. McKertnan, Signe-Mary, Caroline Ratcliffe, Steuerte C. Eugene, Qakenbush Caleb, and Kalish Emma. 2017. "Nine Charts about Wealth Inequality in America Updated," Urban Institute, http://urbn.is/wealthcharts, accessed November 10, 2017.

8. Cocco, Federica. 2017. "Most US Manufacturing Jobs Lost to Technology,

Not Trade," *Financial Times*, https://www.ft.com/content/dec677c0-b7e6-11e6-ba85-95d1533d9a62, accessed November 10, 2017.

9. Witsman Katherine and Ryan Baugh. 2016. "US Naturalizations: 2015," Department of Homeland Security, Office of Immigration Statistics, https://www.dhs.gov/sites/default/files/publications/Naturalizations_2015.pdf, accessed November 11, 2017.

10. Baugh, Ryan and Witsman Katherine. 2017. "US Lawful Permanent Residents: 2015," Department of Homeland Security, Office of Immigration Statistics, https://www.dhs.gov/sites/default/files/publications/Lawful_Permanent_Residents_2015.pdf, accessed November 12, 2017.

11. Krogstad, Jens Manuel, and Richard Fry. 2014. "Department of Education Projects Public Schools Will Be 'Majority-Minority' This Fall," Pew Research Center, http://www.pewresearch.org/fact-tank/2014/08/18/u-s-public-schools-expected-to-be-majority-minority-starting-this-fall/, accessed November 11, 2017.

12. Brown, A. 2015. "Key Takeaways on US Immigration: Past, Present and Future," Pew Research Center, http://www.pewresearch.org/fact-tank/2015/09/28/key-takeaways-on-u-s-immigration-past-present-and-future/, accessed November 11, 2017.

13. López, Gustavo and Jynnah Radford. 2017. "Facts on US Immigrants, 2015: Statistical Portrait of the Foreign-born Population in the United States," Pew Research Center's Hispanic Trends Project, http://www.pewhispanic.org/2017/05/03/facts-on-u-s-immigrants/, accessed November 11, 2017.

14. Rank, Mark R., Kirk A. Foster, and Thomas A. Hirschl. *Chasing the American Dream*. (New York: Oxford University Press, 2014).

15. McCormick, John. 2015. "Nearly Half of Youth Say 'American Dream' Is Dead: Harvard Poll," Bloomberg Politics, https://www.bloomberg.com/news/articles/2015-12-10/nearly-half-of-youth-say-american-dream-is-dead-harvard-poll, accessed November 17, 2017).

16. Officer, Esther B. 2015. "Pew Survey Shows Americans' Financial Worries Cloud Optimism," Pew Charitable Trusts, http://bit.ly/1824qOG, accessed November 12, 2017.

17. McCormick, "Nearly Half of Youth Say 'American Dream' Is Dead."

18. Mehlman, Bruce. "Navigating the New Gilded Age: Why Change Is Coming Again," Mehlman Castagnetti, http://mehlmancastagnetti.com/wp-content/uploads/Mehlman-New-Gilded-Age-Q4-2017.pdf, accessed November 17, 2017.

2. IF TRUTH BE TOLD

1. Liu, Louise. 2016. "Here's Where Hillary Clinton and Donald Trump Stand on Immigration," *Business Insider*, http://www.businessinsider.com/hillary-clinton-and-donald-trump-immigration-2016-9, accessed December 17, 2018.

2. Staff Writer. 2013. "Origins of the Federal Immigration Service," US Customs and Immigration Services, https://www.uscis.gov/history-and-genealogy/our-history/agency-history/origins-federal-immigration-service, accessed November 18, 2017.

3. Staff Writer, 2013. "Refugee Timeline, 2013," US Customs and Immigration

Services, https://www.uscis.gov/history-and-genealogy/our-history/refugee-timeline, accessed November 18, 2017.

4. Staff Writer, 2013. "Refugee Timeline, 2013."

5. Researchers. 2017. Wikipedia, "List of Sovereign States and Dependent Territories by Immigrant Population," https://en.wikipedia.org/w/index.php?title=List_of_sovereign_states_and_dependent_territories_by_immigrant_population&oldid=808641140, accessed November 19, 2017.

6. Staff Writer. 2016. "US Immigration Trends," Migration Policy Institute, https://www.migrationpolicy.org/programs/data-hub/us-immigration-trends, accessed January 2, 2018.

7. Staff Researcher, "US Immigration Trends," Migration Policy Institute.

8. Brown, Anna. 2015. "Key Takeaways on US Immigration: Past, Present and Future," Pew Research Center, http://www.pewresearch.org/fact-tank/2015/09/28/key-takeaways-on-u-s-immigration-past-present-and-future/, accessed December 18, 2017.

9. Brown, "Key Takeaways on US Immigration."

10. Jiménez, Tomás R. 2011. "Immigrants in the United States: How Well Are They Integrating into Society?," Migration Policy Institute, https://www.migrationpolicy.org/research/immigrants-united-states-how-well-are-they-integrating-society, accessed December 18, 2017.

11. Logan, John R. and Brian J. Stults. 2012. "The Persistence of Segregation in the Metropolis: New Findings," Census Project 2010, http://www.s4.brown.edu/us2010h, accessed March 8, 2018.

12. Nicholson, M. D. 2017. "The Facts on Immigration Today: 2017 Edition," *American Progress,* https://www.americanprogress.org/issues/immigration/reports/2017/04/20/430736/facts-immigration-today-2017-edition/, accessed March 8, 2018.

13. Jiménez, "Immigrants in the United States."

14. Weeks, Matthew W. 2017. "UGA Report: Minority Groups Driving US Economy," University of Georgia, Terry Center, http://www.terry.uga.edu/news/releases/uga-report-minority-groups-driving-u.s.-economy, accessed December 18, 2017.

15. Staff Writer. 2011. "The New American Fortune 500," Partnership for a New American Economy, http://www.renewoureconomy.org/sites/all/themes/pnae/img/new-american-fortune-500-june-2011.pdf, accessed December 18, 2017.

16. Somerville, William and Madeleine Sumption. *Immigration and the Labor Market: Theory, Evidence, and Policy*. (Manchester, UK: Equality and Human Rights Commission, 2009).

17. Giovanni, Peri. 2007. "Immigrants' Complementarities and Native Wages: Evidence from California," National Bureau of Economic Research, http://www.nber.org/papers/w12956, accessed December 18, 2017.

18. Cohn, D'Vera and Paul Taylor. 2010. "Baby Boomers Approach 65—Glumly," Pew Research Center, http://www.pewsocialtrends.org/2010/12/20/baby-boomers-approach-65-glumly/, accessed December 21, 2017.

19. Dowell, Myers, Stephen Levy, and John Pitkin. "The Contributions of Immigrants and Their Children to the American Workforce and Jobs of the Future," Center for American Progress, http://www.americanprogress.org/wp-content/uploads/2013/06/OurFutureTogetherUpdated.pdf, accessed December 21, 2017.

20. Passel, Jeffrey S. and D'Vera Cohn. 2017. "Unauthorized Immigrant Population Stable for Half a Decade," Pew Research Center, http://www.pewresearch.org/fact-tank/2016/09/21/unauthorized-immigrant-population-stable-for-half-a-decade/, accessed December 18, 2017.

21. Passel and Cohn, "Unauthorized Immigrant Population Stable for Half a Decade."

22. Miroff, Nick. 2017. "Arrests Along Mexico Border Drop Sharply Under Trump, New Statistics Show," *Washington Post*, https://www.washingtonpost.com/world/national-security/arrests-along-mexico-border-drop-sharply-under-trump-new-statistics-show/2017/12/05/743c6b54-d9c7-11e7-b859-fb0995360725_story.html, accessed December 18, 2017.

23. Warren, Robert and Donald Kerwin. 2017. "The 2,000 Mile Wall in Search of a Purpose: Since 2007 Visa Overstays Have Outnumbered Undocumented Border Crossers by a Half Million," *Journal on Migration and Human Security* 5, no. 1. (2017): 124–136, http://jmhs.cmsny.org/index.php/jmhs/article/*view*/77, accessed December 18, 2017.

24. Staff Writer. 2017. "Southwest Border Migration," US Customs and Border Protection, https://www.cbp.gov/newsroom/stats/sw-border-migration, accessed April 2017.

25. Fitz, Marshall. 2011. "Southwest Border Migration Safer than Ever: A View from the US–Mexico Border: Assessing the Past, Présent, and Future," Center for American Progress, http://www.americanprogress.org/wp-content/uploads/issues/2011/08/pdf/safer_than_ever_report.pdf; accessed April 18, 2017.

26. Staff Writer. 2016. "US Unauthorized Immigration Population Estimates," Pew Research Center, http://www.pewhispanic.org/interactives/unauthorized-immigrants/, accessed April 18, 2017.

27. Staff Writer, "US Unauthorized Immigration Population Estimates."

28. Passel and Cohn, "Unauthorized Immigrant Population Stable for Half a Decade," accessed December 18, 2017.

29. Mathema, Silva. 2015. "Assessing the Economic Impacts of Granting Deferred Action through DACA and DAPA," Center for American Progress, 2015, https://www.americanprogress.org/issues/immigration/news/2015/04/02/110045/assessing-the-economic-impacts-of-granting-deferred-action-through-daca-and-dapa/, accessed January 24, 2018.

30. Goss, Stephen. 2013. "Effects of Unauthorized Immigration on the Actuarial Status of the Social Security Trust Funds," Social Security Administration, https://www.ssa.gov/oact/NOTES/pdf_notes/note151.pdf, accessed December 27, 2017.

31. Zallman, Leah. 2016. "Unauthorized Immigrants Prolong the Life of Medicare's Trust Fund," *Journal of General Internal Medicine* 3, no. 1. (2016): 67–77, http://link.springer.com/article/10.1007/s11606-015-3418-z, accessed December 27, 2017.

32. Gee, Lisa Christensen. 2017. "Undocumented Immigrants' State and Local Tax Contributions," Institute on Taxation and Economic Policy, http://www.itep.org/pdf/immigration2017.pdf, accessed December 18, 2017.

33. Edwards, Ryan and Francesc Ortega. "The Economic Impacts of Removing Unauthorized Immigrant Workers," Center for American Progress, https://www.americanprogress.org/issues/immigration/reports/2016/09/21/144363/the

-economic-impacts-of-removing-unauthorized-immigrant-workers/, accessed March 11, 2018.

34. Staff. 2012. "Deferred Action for Childhood Arrivals (DACA)," Department of Homeland Security, https://www.dhs.gov/topic/deferred-action-childhood-arrivals -daca, accessed March 11, 2018.

35. Krogstad, Jens Manuel. 2017. "DACA Has Shielded Nearly 790,000 Young Unauthorized Immigrants from Deportation," Pew Research Center, http://www .pewresearch.org/fact-tank/2017/09/01/unauthorized-immigrants-covered-by-daca -face-uncertain-future/, accessed January 26, 2018.

36. Zong, Jie, Ariel G. Ruiz Soto, Jeanne Batalova, Julia Gelatt, and Randy Capps. 2017. "A Profile of Current DACA Recipients by Education, Industry, and Occupation," Migration Policy Institute, https://www.migrationpolicy.org/research /profile-current-daca-recipients-education-industry-and-occupation, accessed November 15, 2017.

37. López, Gustavo and Jens Manuel Krogstad. 2017. "Key Facts about Unauthorized Immigrants Enrolled in DACA," Pew Research Center, http://www .pewresearch.org/fact-tank/2017/09/25/key-facts-about-unauthorized-immigrants -enrolled-in-daca/, accessed December 18, 2017.

38. López and Krogstad, "Key Facts about Unauthorized Immigrants Enrolled in DACA."

39. Duke, E. C. 2017. "Memorandum on Rescission of DACA," Department of Homeland Security, https://www.dhs.gov/news/2017/09/05/memorandum -rescission-daca, accessed December 18, 2017.

40. Zong, et al., "A Profile of Current DACA Recipients by Education, Industry, and Occupation."

41. Brannon, Ike and Logan Albright. 2017. "The Economic and Fiscal Impact of Repealing DACA," Cato Institute, https://www.cato.org/blog/economic-fisca l-impact-repealing-daca, accessed April 24, 2017.

42. Wong, Tom K., Greisa Martinez Rosas, Adrian Reyna, Ignacia Rodriguez, Patrick O'Shea, Tom Jawetz, and Philip E. Wolgin. 2016. "New Study of DACA Beneficiaries Shows Positive Economic and Educational Outcomes," Center for American Progress, 2016, https://www.americanprogress.org/issues/immigration /news/2016/10/18/146290/new-study-of-daca-beneficiaries-shows-positive -economic-and-educational-outcomes/, accessed August 12, 2017.

43. Magaña-Salgado, Jose. 2016. "Money on the Table: The Economic Cost of Ending DACA," Immigrant Legal Resource Center, https://www.ilrc.org/sites /default/files/resources/2016-12-13_ilrc_report_-_money_on_the_table_economic _costs_of_ending_daca.pdf, accessed December 18, 2017.

44. Magaña-Salgado, Jose, "Money on the Table."

45. McCarthy, Justin. 2017. "Overall US Desire to Decrease Immigration Unchanged in 2017," Gallup, http://news.gallup.com/poll/212846/overall-desire -decrease-immigration-unchanged-2017.aspx, accessed December 20, 2017.

46. Swift, Art. 2017. "More Americans Say Immigrants Help Rather Than Hurt Economy," Gallup, http://news.gallup.com/poll/213152/americans-say-immigrants -help-rather-hurt-economy.aspx, accessed December 21, 2017.

47. Swift, "More Americans Say Immigrants Help Rather Than Hurt Economy."

48. Swift, "More Americans Say Immigrants Help Rather Than Hurt Economy."

3. THE NATION'S IMMIGRATION LAW

1. Samuelson, Kate. 2017. "Read President Trump's Full Statement on Rescinding DACA," *Time*, http://time.com/4927495/donald-trump-statement-daca-rescind/, accessed January 4, 2018.

2. Capps, Randy and Michael Fix, and Jie Zong. 2017. "The Education and Work Profiles of the DACA Population," Migration Policy Institute, https://www.migrationpolicy.org/research/education-and-work-profiles-daca-population, accessed November 4, 2017.

3. Tarrance, Lance. 2017. "Can a 'Nation of Immigrants' Reform 21st-Century Immigration?" Gallup, http://news.gallup.com/opinion/polling-matters/205304/nation-immigrants-reform-21st-century-immigration.aspx, accessed January 9, 2018.

4. There were two earlier laws that restricted immigration of specific groups. The Naturalization Act of 1790 prohibited the naturalization of nonwhite subjects, not specific ethnic groups. The first federal law limiting immigration qualitatively was enacted in 1875, prohibiting the admission of criminals and prostitutes. The following year the Supreme Court ruled that the regulation of immigration was the sole responsibility of the federal government. In 1891, Congress established the Immigration Service and assumed the responsibility for processing all immigrants seeking admission to the United States.

5. There has always been a racial undertone in our nation's discussion of migration, and anxiety about the racial and ethnic character of immigrants and how they might upset the demographic mix of our society. The Naturalization Act of 1790 provided the first rules guiding the granting of national citizenship, and it limited naturalization to immigrants who were free white persons of good character. It was not until the passage of the Immigration and Nationality Act of 1952 when Congress abolished the racial restrictions found in our immigration laws going back to the 1790 act. The 1952 act retained a quota system for nationalities and regions, but it placed greater importance on labor qualifications. It was not until passage of the Immigration and Nationality Act of 1965 that the quota system ended, and it represents a radical break from the immigration policies of the past. It eliminated national origin, race, and ancestry as the basis for immigration, and gave priority to relatives of US citizens and legal permanent residents and professionals and other individuals with specialized skills. During the signing of the bill, President Johnson remarked the act would not affect the demographic character of this society. He was wrong. The reality is that it marked the beginning of the fourth major wave of immigration; but this time the source of US immigration shifted from Europe to the Americas and Asia, and the demographic character of US society has profoundly changed.

6. Cohn, D'Vera. 2015. "How US Immigration Laws and Rules Have Changed through History," Pew Research Center, http://www.pewresearch.org/fact-tank/2015/09/30/how-u-s-immigration-laws-and-rules-have-changed-through-history/, accessed May 15, 2017.

7. Zong, Jie and Jeanne Batalova. 2017. "Frequently Requested Statistics on Immigrants and Immigration in the United States, Migration Policy Institute, https://www.migrationpolicy.org/article/frequently-requested-statistics-immigrants-and-immigration-united-states, accessed February 10, 2018 and January 9, 2018.

8. Zong and Batalova, "Frequently Requested Statistics on Immigrants and Immigration in the United States.

9. Mittelstadt, Michelle. 2013. "Key Immigration Laws and Policy Developments since 1986," Migration Policy Institute, http://www.migrationpolicy.org/research/timeline-1986, accessed May 15, 2017.

10. The *Plyler* decision involved a 1975 law enacted by the Texas State Legislature that authorized local school districts to bar undocumented children from enrolling in public schools if they chose to do so. The Tyler Independent School District chose to charge these children tuition. In 1977, defense attorneys filed a class action suit against the school district on behalf of these children, and federal courts ruled in 1977 and 1980 that the state law violated the Equal Protection Clause of the Fourteenth Amendment. After a federal appeals court upheld the district court rulings in 1981, the Tyler School Board and school superintendent James Plyler appealed to the Supreme Court. For an excellent overview of the legal background of the DREAM Act and the law behind educating the undocumented, see: Vicky J. Salinas, "You Can Be Whatever You Want to Be When You Grow up, Unless Your Parents Brought You to This Country Illegally: The Struggle to Grant in-State Tuition to Undocumented Immigrant Students," *Houston Law Review* 43 (2006): 847–77.

11. Mittelstadt, "Key Immigration Laws and Policy Developments since 1986."

12. Tarrance, "Can a 'Nation of Immigrants' Reform 21st-Century Immigration?"

13. Batalova, Jeanne, Ariel B. Ruiz Soto, Sarah Pierce, and Randy Capps. 2017. "Differing Dreams: Estimating the Unauthorized Populations That Could Benefit Under Different Legalization Bills," Migration Policy Institute, https://www.migrationpolicy.org/research/differing-dreams-estimating-unauthorized-populations-could-benefit-under-different, accessed January 9, 2018.

14. Frustrated by congressional gridlock, states took up the plight of DREAMers and passed their own laws that provided in-state tuition to undocumented youth. Most laws had a residency requirement and the applicant had to have graduated from a state high school. I wrote about it in chapter 6, "The DREAM Act: Nuts and Bolts," in my 2013 book, *Right to DREAM: Immigration Reform and America's Future.* At the time of the book's release in July 2013, fourteen states had laws or policies permitting certain undocumented students who have graduated from their high schools to pay in-state tuition. The states were California, Connecticut, Illinois, Kansas, Maryland, Nebraska, New Mexico, New York, Oklahoma, Texas, Utah, and Washington. In addition, Rhode Island's Board of Governors for Higher Education voted unanimously to provide access to in-state tuition, regardless of immigration status, beginning in 2012. In November 2012, Massachusetts' governor issued an executive order granting undocumented youth in-state tuition as soon as they received worker permits through deferred action. California has by far the largest number (28.7 percent) of potential beneficiaries, followed by Texas (13.7 percent), Florida (8.7 percent), Arizona (6.3 percent), and New York (4.1 percent). Together, they account for 62 percent of those eligible for relief under the DREAM Act.

15. The only exception was President William Henry Harrison. He didn't have the opportunity. He was suffering from pneumonia the day he took office and died thirteen days later.

16. Staff Writer. 2018. "The American Presidency Project—Executive Orders,"

American Presidency Project, http://www.presidency.ucsb.edu/data/orders.php, assessed January 9, 2018.

17. See chapter 6, "The DREAM Act: Nuts and Bolts," in William A. Schwab, *Right to DREAM: Immigration Reform and America's Future*. (Fayetteville: University of Arkansas Press. 2013).

18. On January 9, 2018, the United States District Court for the Northern District of California issued a preliminary injunction against the government's rescission of the DACA (Case 3:17-cv-05211-WHA Document 234 Filed 01/09/18). In response to the injunction, the US Citizenship and Immigration Services announced on January 13, 2018, they would begin accepting DACA requests for renewal. The Senate could not pass a bill, and there was a partial federal government shutdown; see: https://www.uscis.gov/humanitarian/deferred-action-childhood-arrivals-response-january-2018-preliminary-injunction, accessed January 10, 2018.

19. DeMarche, Edmund. 2018. "Judge Rules against Trump Administration on Rescinding DACA," Fox News, http://www.foxnews.com/politics/2018/01/10/judge-rules-against-trump-administration-on-rescinding-daca.html, accessed March 7, 2018.

20. Staff Writer. 2017. "Frequently Asked Questions: Rescission of Deferred Action for Childhood Arrivals (DACA)," Department of Homeland Security, https://www.dhs.gov/news/2017/09/05/frequently-asked-questions-rescission-deferred-action-childhood-arrivals-daca, accessed January 9, 2018.

21. Staff Writer. 2015. "A Guide to Children Arriving at the Border: Laws, Policies and Responses," American Immigration Council, https://www.americanimmigrationcouncil.org/research/guide-children-arriving-border-laws-policies-and-responses, assessed January 1, 2018.

22. Somerville, William and Madeleine Sumption. *Immigration and the Labor Market: Theory, Evidence, and Policy*. (Manchester, UK: Equality and Human Rights Commission, 2009).

23. Giovanni, Peri. 2007. "Immigrants' Complementarities and Native Wages: Evidence from California," National Bureau of Economic Research, http://www.nber.org/papers/w12956, accessed Jan 12, 2018.

24. Blau F. D. and C. Mackie, eds. *The Economic and Fiscal Consequences of Immigration* (Washington, DC: The National Academies Press, 2017).

25. Wong, Tom K., Greisa Martinez Rosas, Adrian Reyna, Ignacia Rodriguez, Patrick O'Shea, Tom Jawetz, and Philip E. Wolgin. 2016 . "New Study of DACA Beneficiaries Shows Positive Economic and Educational Outcomes," Center for American Progress, 2016, https://www.americanprogress.org/issues/immigration/news/2016/10/18/146290/new-study-of-daca-beneficiaries-shows-positive-economic-and-educational-outcomes/, accessed August 12, 2017.

26. Landgrave, Michelangelo and Alex Nowrasteh. 2017. "Criminal Immigrants: Their Numbers, Demographics, and Countries of Origin," Cato Institute, https://www.cato.org/publications/immigration-reform-bulletin/criminal-immigrants-their-numbers-demographics-countries, accessed January 12, 2018.

27. Landgrave and Nowrasteh, "Criminal Immigrants."

28. Gates, Gary J. 2017. "US Satisfaction with Immigration Levels Reaches New High," Gallup, http://news.gallup.com/poll/202541/satisfaction-immigration-levels-reaches-new-high.aspx, accessed December 21, 2017.

29. Brannon, Ike and Logan Albright. 2017. "The Economic and Fiscal Impact of Repealing DACA," Cato Institute, https://www.cato.org/blog/economic-fiscal-impact-repealing-daca, accessed April 24, 2017.

4. DACA BY THE NUMBERS

1. After receiving DACA in 2013, Jazmin was able to graduate with an master of science in physics from the University of Arkansas in 2015. She spent some time working as a data analyst at a large university in the Midwest before becoming the director of educational programs at a science museum in Indiana, where she gets to indulge in her love of all things space- and tech-related. Jazmin is active in her new community, working to build support networks for undocumented, DACAmented, and documented immigrants, advocating for people of color and searching for the best Mexican food in the Midwest.

2. US Immigration and Customs Enforcement (ICE) data show that the Obama administration deported a monthly average of 32,886 people, significantly higher than the 20,964 removals during the Bush administration. Bill Clinton was far behind with 9,059 removals per month. All previous occupants of the White House going back to 1892 fell well short of the level of the three past presidents. The Trump administration so far lags behind with 16,900 removals per month. Therefore, the Obama administration deported more undocumented immigrants than any other administration. See ICE removal statistics at https://www.ice.gov/statistics.

3. Krogstad, Jens Manuel. 2017. "DACA Has Shielded Nearly 790,000 Young Unauthorized Immigrants from Deportation," Pew Research Center, http://www.pewresearch.org/fact-tank/2017/09/01/unauthorized-immigrants-covered-by-daca-face-uncertain-future/, accessed January 26, 2018.

4. Agency Staff. 2018. "Data Set: Form I-821D Deferred Action for Childhood Arrivals," US Citizenship and Immigration Services, https://www.uscis.gov/tools/reports-studies/immigration-forms-data/data-set-form-i-821d-deferred-action-childhood-arrivals, accessed January 27, 2018.

5. López, Gustavo and Jens Manuel Krogstad. 2017. "Key Facts about Unauthorized Immigrants Enrolled in DACA," Pew Research Center, http://www.pewresearch.org/fact-tank/2017/09/25/key-facts-about-unauthorized-immigrants-enrolled-in-dac/, accessed December 18, 2017.

6. Batalova, Jeanne, Ariel B. Ruiz Soto, Sarah Pierce, and Randy Capps. 2017. "Differing Dreams: Estimating the Unauthorized Populations That Could Benefit Under Different Legalization Bills," Migration Policy Institute, https://www.migrationpolicy.org/research/differing-dreams-estimating-unauthorized-populations-could-benefit-under-different, accessed November 4, 2017.

7. See table 4.1 for the details on each legislative proposal in Batalova, Jeanne, Ariel B. Ruiz Soto, and Michelle Mittelstadt. (2017). "Protecting the DREAM: The Potential Impact of Different Legislative Scenarios for Unauthorized Youth," Migration Policy Institute Fact Sheet, https://www.migrationpolicy.org/research/protecting-dream-potential-impact-different-legislative-scenarios-unauthorized-youth, accessed November 4, 2017.

For charts and an infograph on the legislation see Batalova, Jeanne, Ariel B.

Ruiz Soto, Sarah Pierce, and Randy Capps. 2017. "Differing Dreams: Estimating the Unauthorized Populations that could Benefit Under Different Legalization Bills," Migration Policy Institute, https://www.migrationpolicy.org/research/differing-dreams-estimating-unauthorized-populations-could-benefit-under-different (accessed December 18, 2018).

8. López and Krogstad, "Key Facts about Unauthorized Immigrants Enrolled in DACA."

9. López and Krogstad, "Key Facts about Unauthorized Immigrants Enrolled in DACA."

10. Capps, Randy Michael Fix, and Jie Zong. 2017. "The Education and Work Profiles of the DACA Population," Migration Policy Institute, https://www.migrationpolicy.org/research/education-and-work-profiles-daca-population, accessed November 4, 2017.

11. Zong, Jie, Ariel G. Ruiz Soto, Jeanne Batalova, Julia Gelatt, and Randy Capps. 2017. "A Profile of Current DACA Recipients by Education, Industry, and Occupation," Migration Policy Institute, https://www.migrationpolicy.org/research/profile-current-daca-recipients-education-industry-and-occupation, accessed November 15, 2017.

12. López and Krogstad, "Key Facts about Unauthorized Immigrants Enrolled in DACA."

13. This was the largest study to date of DACA recipients with a sample size of 3,063 respondents in forty-six states as well as the District of Columbia. Based on a scientifically drawn sample, researchers can generalize from the sample to the population of DACA recipients with a known degree of error.

14. Kurtzleben, Danielle. 2017. "Fact Check: Are DACA Recipients Stealing Jobs Away from Other Americans?" National Public Radio, http://www.npr.org/2017/09/06/548882071/fact-check-are-daca-recipients-stealing-jobs-away-from-other-americans, accessed November 4, 2017.

15. Patler, Caitlin and Jorge A. Cabrera. *From Undocumented to DACAmented: Impacts of the Deferred Action for Childhood Arrivals (DADA) Program*. (Los Angeles: UCLA Press, Chicano Studies, 2016).

16. Agency Staff. 2012. "Deferred Action for Childhood Arrivals (DACA)," Department of Homeland Security, https://www.dhs.gov/archive/deferred-action-childhood-arrivals, accessed December 18, 2017.

17. Mittelstadt, Michelle. 2017. "DACA Holders Set to Begin Losing Protections in Growing Numbers New March, Reaching an Average of 915 Per Day through March 2020," Migration Policy Institute, https://www.migrationpolicy.org/news/daca-holders-set-begin-losing-protections-growing-numbers-next-march-reaching-average-915-day, accessed December 18, 2017.

18. Agency Staff. 2017. "Frequently Asked Questions: Rescission of Deferred Action for Childhood Arrivals (DACA)," Department of Homeland Security, https://www.dhs.gov/news/2017/09/05/frequently-asked-questions-rescission-deferred-action-childhood-arrivals-daca, accessed December 18, 2017.

19. Deputy Director Homan, Thomas D. 2018. "Civil Immigration Enforcement Inside Courthouses," US Immigration and Customs Enforcement, https://www.ice.gov/sites/default/files/documents/Document/2018/ciEnforcementActionsCourthouses.pdf, accessed January 24, 2018.

20. Brannon, Ike and Albright, Logan. 2017. "The Economic and Fiscal Impact of Repealing DACA," Cato Institute, https://www.cato.org/blog/economic-fiscal-impact-repealing-daca, accessed April 24, 2017.

21. Brannon and Logan. "The Economic and Fiscal Impact of Repealing DACA."

22. Magaña-Salgado, Jose and Tom K. Wong. *Draining the Trust Funds: Ending DACA and the Consequences to Social Security and Medicare.* (San Francisco: Immigration Legal Resource Center, 2017).

23. See what the ending of DACA will cost your state. Svajlenka, Nicole Prchal, Tom Jawetz, and Angie Bautista-Chavez. 2017. "A New Threat to DACA Could Cost States Billions of Dollars," Center for American Progress, https://www.americanprogress.org/issues/immigration/news/2017/07/21/436419/new-threat-daca-cost-states-billions-dollars/, accessed February 4, 2018.

24. Austin, John C. 2018. "Losing Dreamers Would Be a Loss for Heartland Economy," Brookings Institute, https://www.brookings.edu/blog/the-avenue/2018/01/31/losing-dreamers-would-be-a-loss-for-heartland-economy/, accessed February 2, 2018.

25. Fox, Vicente. 2018. "If Trump Doesn't Want DACA, Mexico Will Take All of Them," Twitter, https://twitter.com/attn/status/956943070783664128, accessed February 2, 2018.

26. Vasel, Kathryn. 2017. "Cost of Raising a Child: $233,610." *CNN Money,* http://money.cnn.com/2017/01/09/pf/cost-of-raising-a-child-2015/index.html (accessed February 2, 2018).

5. ALLIES

1. My students and I were experiencing firsthand the transformation of the lives of undocumented young people in our region. We wanted to get their voices on video so that future generations could hear their stories. What did the DACA program mean to them? How had their lives changed since receiving protective status, entering the workforce, moving out of the shadow, and fully participating in our society? We wanted to document the emotional roller coaster they experienced since the September 5, 2017, announcement that DACA had ended. How did they feel about the existential threat to all they had accomplished? Was there a sense of betrayal from the only society that they have ever known? We wanted to learn more about the uncertainty that loomed over their future. The stress rescission had had on their marriages, children, and families, the specter of deportation and unemployment, the prospect of moving back into the shadows and back into the underground economy. What were their fears about doing the things associated with the rhythm of daily life such as going to the store, taking the kids to school, going to church, and driving their children to soccer practice and after-school events? What does it feel like to know that jail, a detention center, and deportation was a traffic stop away? We wanted to get a complete story, so we included an array of people, pro and con, on the immigration debate.

2. In January 2018, a federal district court judge stayed Trump administration's executive order to rescind DACA. The Supreme Court has refused the administration's request to by-pass the appellate process, so there has been a reprieve for the

DACAmented and Congress has more time to act. US Citizenship and Immigration Services is once again accepting renewals but not new applications for deferred action.

6. OLD FRIENDS

1. The Cisneros Center, "The Inaugural Program: The American Dream Initiative," San Antonio, Texas.

7. NEXT STEPS

1. I am an American of German ancestry. Our German heritage is part of my family lore and identity. Growing up my father made sauerkraut, sauer turnips (it is as bad as it sounds), and wine. We ate German foods like sauerkraut with pig's tails and feet, German sausage with sweet and sour potato salad, sauerbraten with kartoffel kloesse (potato dumplings) and red cabbage, and goetta (a German breakfast dish made with pork necks and oatmeal but better than it sounds). We lived in the Cincinnati area and my dad would take me to the old Findley Market whose vendors my father had known since his childhood—all of German heritage. My sister, Julie, recently received her DNA story from AncestryDNA. Here are her results—ethnicity regions: Great Britain, 58 percent; Europe South, 13 percent; Scandinavia, 10 percent; Europe West (Germany and the Midwestern United States), 6 percent; the Iberian Peninsula 6 percent; and five other regions. Migrations: Pennsylvania settlers. Benjamin Franklin, maybe the English were better at Anglifying the Germans than you thought. And now I know why I'm drawn to the Dreamers. We share a common ancestry—I'm 6 percent German and 6 percent Iberian Peninsula! I would love to see the AncestryDNA of the leadership in the anti-immigrant movement. Could they be in for an existential crisis?

2. Yglesias, Matthew. 2008. "Swarty Germans," *The Atlantic*, https://www.theatlantic.com/politics/archive/2008/02/swarthy-germans/48324/, accessed February 8, 2017.

3. Rampell, Catherine. 2015. "Founding Fathers, Trashing Immigrants," *Washington Post*, https://www.washingtonpost.com/news/rampage/wp/2015/08/28/founding-fathers-trashing-immigrants/?utm_term=.15dbd1bba5f0, accessed February 8, 2017.

4. Washington, H. A. *Writings of Thomas Jefferson: Being His Autobiography, Correspondence, Reports, Messages, Addresses, and Other Writings, Official and Private.* (Washington, DC: Taylor and Maury, 1854), p. 84.

5. Cohn, D'Vera. 2015. "How US Immigration Laws and Rules Have Changed through History," Pew Research Center, http://www.pewresearch.org/fact-tank/2015/09/30/how-u-s-immigration-laws-and-rules-have-changed-through-history/, accessed May 15, 2017.

6. Cowger, Sela, Jessica Bolter, and Sarah Pierce. 2017. "The First 100 Days: Summary of Major Immigration Actions Taken by the Trump Administration," Migration Policy Institute, https://www.migrationpolicy.org/research/first-100

-days-summary-major-immigration-actions-taken-trump-administration, accessed November 4, 2017.

7. Harrington, Rebecca. 2017. "Trump Has Already Signed 78 Executive Actions—Here's What Each One Does," *Business Insider*, http: / / www.business insider.com / trump-executive-orders-memorandum-proclamations-presidential -action-guide-2017-1, accessed April 28, 2017.

8. Gonzalez-Barrera, Ana. 2016. "Apprehensions of Mexican Migrants at US Borders Reach Near-Historic Low," Pew Research Center, http: / / www.pewresearch .org / fact-tank / 2016 / 04 / 14 / mexico-us-border-apprehensions / , accessed February 26, 2018.

9. Cowger, Bolter, and Pierce. "The First 100 Days."

10. Anderson, Nick. 2017. "Report Finds Fewer New International Students on US College Campuses," *Washington Post,* https: / / www.washingtonpost.com / local / education / report-finds-fewer-new-international-students-on-us-college-campuses / 2017 / 11 / 12 / 5933fe02-c61d-11e7-aae0-cb18a8c29c65_story.html, accessed February 26, 2018.

11. Calder, Simon. 2016. "One Million Fewer British Visitors to the US Predicted as Prospective Tourists React to Trump's Victory," *The Independent* (online), November 9, 2016, https: / / search.proquest.com / docview / 1837464856, accessed February 26, 2018.

12. Staff Writer. 2016. "How Donald Trump Affects America's Tourist Business: The Industry's Lobby Wants Him to Reassure Foreign Visitors," *The Economist,* https: / / www.economist.com / news / business / 21721234-industrys-lobby-wants-him -reassure-foreign-visitors-how-donald-trump-affects-americas, accessed February 26, 2018.

123. Wike, Richard, Bruce Stokes, Jacob Poushter, and Janell Fetterolf. 2017. "US Image Suffers as Publics around World Question Trump's Leadership," Pew Research Center, Global Attitudes Project, http: / / www.pewglobal.org / 2017 / 06 / 26 / u-s-image -suffers-as-publics-around-world-question-trumps-leadership / , accessed February 26, 2018.

14. Swift, Art. 2017. "More Americans Say Immigrants Help Rather Than Hurt Economy," Gallup, http: / / news.gallup.com / poll / 213152 / americans-say-immigrants -help-rather-hurt-economy.aspx, accessed December 21, 2017.

15. Reinhart, R. J. 2018. "In the News: Immigration," Gallup, http: / / news.gallup .com / poll / 225200 / news-immigration.aspx, accessed February 26, 2018.

16. The US Census used Baby Boomer, but typically does not define generations or name them. It is our popular culture that attaches the labels like Generation X and Millennials. There is also some debate on what are the starting and ending years of each generation. They tend to be a little fuzzy at the beginning and ending birth years. I've cited the dates used by the Pew Research Center in my analysis.

17. McCarthy, Justin. 2017. "US Support for Gay Marriage Edges to New High," Gallup, http: / / news.gallup.com / poll / 210566 / support-gay-marriage-edges -new-high.aspx, accessed February 28, 2018..

18. Staff Writers. 2015. "Support for Same-Sex Marriage at Record High, but Key Segments Remain Opposed," Pew Research Center, http: / / www.people-press .org / 2015 / 06 / 08 / support-for-same-sex-marriage-at-record-high-but-key-segments -remain-opposed / , accessed February 28, 2018.

19. Intergenerational change will also shape the power of special interest groups. The average age of a white Evangelical Christian is fifty-seven. Twenty-eight percent of Boomers are affiliated with this denomination, and 11 percent are unaffiliated with any religion. In contrast, only 20 percent of Millennials are Evangelical Protestants, and 35 percent are unaffiliated or unchurched. The political influence of this group will wane as their members age and die. The NRA does not release data on the age of its members, but that organization probably faces a similar demographic future.

20. Dimock, Michael. 2018. "Defining Generations: Where Millennials End and Post-Millennials Begin," Pew Research Center, http://www.pewresearch.org/fact-tank/2018/03/01/defining-generations-where-millennials-end-and-post-millennials-begin/, accessed March 2, 2018.

INDEX

Note: Page numbers in italics refer to illustrative material.